A Portrayal of Emily Carr

m.e.

A Portrayal of Emily Carr

Edythe Hembroff-Schleicher

Introduction by Susan Crean

Mother Tongue Publishing Limited
Salt Spring Island, BC
Canada

Copyright ©1969, 2014 Edythe Hembroff-Schleicher

First published in 1969 by Clarke, Irwin & Company Limited.
This edition published 2013 by:

MOTHER TONGUE PUBLISHING LIMITED
290 Fulford–Ganges Road
Salt Spring Island, B.C. V8K 2K6
Canada
phone: 250-537-4155   fax 250-537-4725

Book Design by Mark Hand

Front cover painting: Edythe Hembroff-Schleicher, Portrait of Emily Carr (with griffon dog), 1971,
oil on canvas, 33½" x 27½", Art Gallery of Greater Victoria Collection.
Back cover painting: Edythe Hembroff-Schleicher, Untitled (Edythe with Emily Carr in the door of
her caravan, the Elephant), n.d., oil, photo from Art Gallery of Greater Victoria Collection.
Photo of Edythe Hembroff -Schleicher, p. 77, from the Art Gallery of Greater Victoria Collection.
Typefaces used are Chaparral and Quadon.
Printed on Silva Enviro 106 100% recycled. Certified EcoLogo and processed chlorine free.
Printed and bound in Canada.

Mother Tongue Publishing gratefully acknowledges the assistance of the Province of British Columbia through the
B.C. Arts Council and we acknowledge the support of the Canada Council for the Arts, which last year invested
$157 million in writing and publishing throughout Canada. Nous remercions de son soutien le Conseil des Arts du
Canada, qui a investi 157$ millions de dollars l'an dernier dans les lettres et l'édition à travers le Canada.

LIBRARY AND ARCHIVES CANADA
CATALOGUING IN PUBLICATION

Hembroff-Schleicher, Edythe, author
      M.E. : a portrayal of Emily Carr / Edythe Hembroff-Schleicher ;
introduction by Susan Crean.

Reprint with a new introduction. Originally published: Toronto : Clarke,
      Irwin Co., 1969.
Includes edited versions of 20 letters written by Emily Carr.
ISBN 978-1-896949-33-8 (pbk.)

      1. Carr, Emily, 1871-1945. 2. Carr, Emily, 1871-1945--Mental health.
3. Carr, Emily, 1871-1945--Friends and associates. 4. Painters--British
Columbia--Biography. I. Title. II. Title: Portrayal of Emily Carr.

ND249.C3S3 2014   759.11   C2013-908400-2

CONTENTS

M.E.: A Portrayal of Emily Carr, originally published in 1969, was the first book written about Emily Carr. Her journals, *Hundreds and Thousands*, had come out in 1966, twenty years after her death, and with the rerelease of several titles (notably *Klee Wyck* and *The Book of Small*), stirred up new interest in her life and work. Edythe Hembroff-Schleicher's book was prescient, though she would have known of the attention beginning to be paid Carr by scholars and art critics. Starting with the 1971 exhibition at the Vancouver Art Gallery, the seventies brought a succession of books and articles about Carr, including the major contributions of art historian Doris Shadbolt and biographer Maria Tippett. By comparison, *M.E.* is a simple short text of modest ambitions, a first-person account of the friendship between Hembroff-Schleicher and Carr, centering on their sketching trips together in the early 1930s. Written by a younger artist who Carr considered serious enough to accompany her as a working partner, the book has the value of being an eyewitness account of Carr's artistic process, an inside view of her life roughing it in the woods.

Hembroff-Schleicher calls her book a portrayal, which suggests it's not meant to be the complete picture. Instead it's a description of Carr in her last years as Hembroff-Schleicher knew her, a recreation of their encounter as artists, one beginning her career and one still blossoming in late life. This candid account allows us to see Edythe through Carr's eyes, as well as Carr through hers. Initially, they circled each other, friendship by no means a foregone conclusion. "We were cautiously picking our way into friendship, prodding and parrying to see how much sympathy existed between us." Edythe was in her twenties, Emily pushing sixty, and they were an unlikely duo, not only because they were two generations and an era apart. Hembroff-Schleicher had family support and money behind her, was able to combine marriage with painting and was pals with a number of young male artists Carr disparaged (notably Max Maynard and Jack Shadbolt). But none of this put Carr off. Edythe was an ace camping companion who came with a car and, as she herself notes, access to the family cottage on Cordova Bay that housed them on one trip.

Even if she led a privileged life, Hembroff-Schleicher was clearly up to the task of getting along with Carr. She had a positive disposition, was game and possessed some of the same ingenuity she admired in the older artist. "Carr tackled plumbing, carpentry and stove repairs. She sized and stretched her own canvasses and made her own easels. She once made a cot out of an old moosehide and even made her own soap.... She was practically self-sufficient."

Hembroff-Schleicher offers little commentary on Carr's

work, but a good deal about her personality and her attitudes. They were clearly very different painters. Emily did not take to shoreline and water; Edythe did not take to trees. The book does reveal a side of Carr not often seen—the two of them joking around when Edythe challenges Emily to paint each other's portraits, of Carr playing the role of mentor to a younger woman artist, "[Carr's] only Sketching Partner."

Hembroff-Schleicher was in her sixties when she wrote *M.E.* Carr was known to the general public by then, on her way to becoming a national icon, so the main strokes of the stereotype were set. Some of these are evident in *M.E.*—Carr's short wick and acid tongue, the prudishness, the way with animals, the tortured relations with her sisters and local Victoria arts aficionados. But the rendering is fond, even though Hembroff-Schleicher does not shy from judgment. Rereading the book after twenty-odd years (and writing my own book on Carr), I find there is a freshness in her observations, and that I'd forgotten how well-written it is. For many, *M.E.* was overshadowed by Hembroff-Schleicher's subsequent book, *Emily Carr: The Untold Story*, which was an entirely different proposition. Its central purpose was to set the record straight. Allowing that she is a "non-professional" and wondering if she dared, Hembroff-Schleicher undertook the prodigious task of correcting all the errors she'd found in other people's writings on Carr. This resulted in a four-hundred-page compendium of information about Carr's life and career, including a number of chapters addressing particular controversies. Inevitably, Emily herself becomes a chief culprit with her changing versions of events and straying from the "facts," and Edythe the lone defender of the truth.

Both books are essential parts of the historical record on Carr, and immensely valuable as primary source material. Of the two, however, *M.E.* is the more readable, possessing contemporary resonance because we can recognize it as a work of narrative non-fiction. It has lasting value not only as a statement on Carr by someone who knew her, but as a lively memoir of Hembroff-Schleicher's own early years as an artist.

Susan Crean,
Toronto, 2013

Preface

When, as a fledgling artist, I first met Emily Carr, it never occurred to me to call her by her given name. She sometimes objected to this and in one of her letters to me she added a P.S.: "Why don't you and Fred call me other than 'Miss.' Any of my epithets you fancy."

I had a wide choice; at various times she called herself "Emily," "Millie," "Mom," or "M.E." She also signed her pictures in three different ways: "Emily Carr," "M.E. Carr," or "M. Emily Carr."

I asked her once, "What does the 'M' stand for?"

"It doesn't stand for anything," she answered. "I was born just plain Emily. But because I had two older sisters who were both 'E's' [Edith and Elizabeth] I added the 'M' to distinguish myself from them." She didn't say so, but I imagine she took the "M" from her old childhood nickname of "Millie."

The signatures on Emily's painting varied at different times of her life. In early life she used her given name alone. Later she added the "M" and after the death of her sister Lizzie she returned to the unadorned "Emily" again.

Her art, like her signatures, can be divided into three periods. Her earliest work was literal and descriptive, a remarkable record of actual scenes along the British Columbia coast. It possessed both artistic and historic value. But it was not interpretative nor profound.

The second phase came with the use of Indian forms as isolated symbols in the picture, fitted schematically into the setting of rock, village, forest or curve of bay. The living totemic contours and features were retained and blended harmoniously with a stylized environment. She gradually abandoned the Indian theme, but considered that Indian forms had liberated her powers of seeing. This was undoubtedly true; they had set her mind free from the limitations of the actual outlines and shapes to construct the life, the movement, the mood she felt within the forms of nature and the atmosphere. But the actual appearance of the picture was structural and moulded, fold within fold. This process of "abstraction," although too severe a word to apply to her real work, was then carried further, particularly in her charcoal studies of forest scenes and tree forms. Precise geometrical lines and figures made their appearance. Rigidity and something of hard iron entered her composition, and the life of the piece was to be found in the incidental play of light and shadow, almost unrelated to the living original object that was being interpreted.

In her third period, she cast off all these bonds. Her field sketches and the resulting canvases became marvellously lyrical and free.

Whatever period of her work is considered it displays no

falseness. It is genuine and individual. It is Emily Carr. I want to insist on this point because she drilled it into me that the technique would come if the idea was held firmly and clearly in mind. She did not go "modern." Mannerisms in painting, as in living, appalled her. Her aim was the age-old but difficult one: "Be yourself."

As I look back now on the whole canvas of Emily's life, at least on those parts in the middle background where I was destined to take my brush and add a few strokes, I see many highlights but many deep shadows too. The picture of her life is as vital, as original, as full of depth and yearning as any she ever painted. Like the gay little trees in her paintings, the humour in her writing, there were bright spots and fun in her living. There were also dark areas of struggle and despair. It was my privilege to share in both aspects of the composition.

E. Hembroff-Schleicher
Victoria, British Columbia
February, 1969

Chapter One

*I*t was during Emily Carr's middle period, her "blue period" as she sometimes called it, that I entered her life. More accurately speaking, it was then that she entered mine. I had just returned to Victoria after two years' study in art schools abroad and there was a little write-up about my training there and in San Francisco in the local newspapers. I had scarcely settled down with my family when I was called to the telephone.

"This is Emily Carr speaking. I saw your picture in the paper and your study experiences are an exact echo of mine of so long ago. Come to my studio and let's reminisce. Better still, come to a little garden-party I'm having on Saturday and we'll get acquainted."

I was puzzled but accepted. Who was Emily Carr? Why, if she was an artist, had I heard nothing of her? Today I acknowledge with shame that her name was unfamiliar to me until that spring of 1930. But I had been away from Victoria for five years and before that few people discussed Emily or her art. If she was mentioned at all, it was probably as "that grumpy old landlady on Simcoe Street who makes Indian pottery in her back yard and raises sheep dogs."

Perhaps people did not even realize that Emily Carr was an artist. Her brushes had lain completely idle for fifteen years while she devoted all her strength to squeezing a thin living out of a house of apartments, and she had only recently taken them up again. Those who had known her when she held an exhibition on her return from France in 1911 had probably long since forgotten the event and the shocked scorn with which her "outlandish" modern pictures were received.

"Artist Returns from Europe," from news clipping about Edythe, 1930, from the Art Gallery of Greater Victoria Collection

Years before, when my parents had thought they saw promise in my early drawings and sought a teacher to develop my talent, Emily Carr's name was not even mentioned. A great artist's energies were being squandered in tussles with tenants while I learned to do conventional little landscapes and flower studies. My teacher was an amiable lady, Miss Marjory Kitto, who had gained a considerable reputation for her paintings of Beacon Hill broom which were widely reproduced and sold as pretty postcards. Though her house was just across the park from Miss Carr's they lived poles apart, in completely different art climates. It was my great loss that my parents, who could have sent me to a fine artist and stimulating teacher, in all innocence sent me to the wrong side of the park.

As the day of the visit approached I became excited. I had not expected to find many real artists or real studios in Victoria but, judging from the bits of gossip I had picked up and pieced together since Miss Carr's call, I was sure I was going to meet at least one. I put on my smartest Paris frock and drove through town to James Bay. I turned into Simcoe. There it was—646, the dwelling that Emily called the House of All Sorts. It looked ordinary enough, just a brown box sitting conventionally in a small garden. There was nothing to distinguish it from its neighbours. I felt somehow that an artist should have shown more originality in building, that a studio window or skylight should be visible from the street. Slightly disappointed, I walked around the house to the garden and was greeted by a chorus of sharp yaps from a crowd of strange little brown dogs which tried their best to be ferocious, snorting and snuffling around my ankles.

"Down, Koko. Down, Koko!"

The dogs obediently sat on their haunches, growling just a little to show that they were still on the alert. The speaker approached. There she was—Emily Carr who was to play such an important role in my life for the next decade and more!

On this occasion, dressed up for a party, she did not appear odd. She looked, in fact, very much like a comfortable housewife. She had on a plain black dress, obviously home-made, which covered her ample figure like a nightgown with no attempt at line or form. She wore no jewellery or ornament of any kind, and her shoes were stout, shabby black oxfords. She had a pleasant, fresh, round face under the severe line of a headband from which unruly wisps of hair escaped, a small mouth, a delicate nose and really astonishing slanted blue-gray eyes with heavy, arched, dark eyebrows. There was about her an air of great vitality.

Miss Carr's voice was pleasant and warm as she greeted me. She put me at my ease at once. I was introduced to the guests— an assorted group. There was a smartly dressed woman from Vancouver, two old ladies who were longstanding friends of the Carr family, Emily's sister Alice, one of the House of All Sorts tenants, and a lone young man—an artist—who tried desperately to keep the conversation on an intellectual level. Miss Carr, who was obviously not interested in aesthetics and the history of art, listened politely but vaguely to snatches of the young man's lecture on Picasso and Roger Fry. The rest of us knew too little to follow the lead, and the conversation quickly degenerated to dogs.

As a matter of fact, the party seemed to centre around Emily's animals. The sheep dogs that she had raised for many years had by then been replaced by the little Belgian griffons which had greeted me so noisily. Koko was the veteran of the lot and the favourite but there were always three or four others, assorted "roughs" and "smooths." Her pet monkey, Woo, was there in a starring role, demanding attention with constant chattering. Woo was dressed in her best pinafore and was chained to the leg of the tea-table to keep her out of mischief. She accepted tidbits graciously with her dainty little black fingers and stored up the reserve supply in her jowl pockets until they were puffed out like balloons. As periodic distraction, she combed the grass energetically in search of ants. Susie, a white rat, was there too. She stayed in her cage during tea but later she was given a perch on Emily's shoulder where she roamed at will, sometimes poking her nose under the neckline of the dress.

The tea went on in between distractions. The tenant, who had been elected helper for the day, kept running up and down the long, treacherous outside steps which led to the studio door on the upper floor, bringing plates of sandwiches and re-fills of tea. Once, when Emily collided with her on the narrow stair and a few cakes went hurtling down to the walk below, Miss Carr called her a very impolite name and scolded her for her carelessness. Although our hostess regained her smiling composure by the time she rejoined us, the unjust outbreak had made its impression on me. On this, my very first visit, I saw that Emily Carr could lose her temper and lash out with her tongue on small provocation; I was warned, and I resolved to be on my guard.

As I sat among the guests at the party, I gazed up occasion-ally at the big studio window overlooking the garden. So there *was* a real studio after all! The street side of the house had been deceptive; it was a false front hiding the secret and real activity of the place. The back, where Emily lived, could have been a studio in any large art centre. The big artist's window, the hig-geldy-piggeldy stairs clinging precariously to the outside walk, the pots of paint and turpentine on the landing and the huge gray Persian cat, Adolphus, curled up on the railing, all con-tributed to give this part of the house an atmosphere that bore the imprint of the artist's work and personality.

"Miss Carr," I asked timidly, "would it be possible to see your studio and some of your work?"

"No," she said decisively. "This is a party and nobody wants to bother with my paintings today. Come by yourself some time next week and we'll have a talk and a show."

In a few days I was back, eager to see how Emily Carr lived and worked. The big high studio was such a clutter of pictures, furniture, painting materials and domestic odds and ends that I was only able to sort out my impressions slowly. There was a cleared space around an open stove in one corner which served as a sitting-room. There was a couch along one wall where I sat and, on the other side of the stove, a wooden armchair which Emily and the pile of dogs on her lap completely filled. A few other chairs hung from the ceiling, each with its own pulley, ready to be swung down into place when more people were expected. The space near the window was partitioned off with furniture and boxes to make a painting nook and two canvases stood facing each other on crude home-made easels, both draped to prevent the curious from seeing unfinished work. A huge table near the entrance was piled high with a confused mass of objects: painting materials, sewing materials, pottery, house and garden tools, etc., and, in the midst, was Susie in her cage. Two chipmunks spun around on a miniature Ferris wheel in another cage nearby. A little stairway in the corner opposite me led to a low attic room where Emily slept. The door was open and I could see part of some dark, stark Indian eagles she had painted on the whitewashed surface of the sloping roof. Reminders of her many trips to paint in Indian villages were everywhere. Besides the eagles, there were numerous pieces of pottery scattered around, all with Indian designs. A hooked rug with Indian design was on the floor and another hung on the wall surrounded by Indian paintings. The walls, the most striking part of the studio, were covered, almost from floor to ceiling, with canvases, sketches, photographs, plaster casts and knicknacks. Here, in one informal exhibition, was the record of Emily's entire painting life.

All this I took in superficially while we were cautiously picking our way into friendship, prodding and parrying to see how much sympathy existed between us, how much common ground. It was like stepping over stones to reach a smooth sandbar beyond. There was the age barrier to overcome (Emily was then 58 years old) and a vast difference in background. Her life had been hard, an uphill fight; mine, so far, had been cushioned. But still, we did have those common experiences in the art schools of San Francisco, London and Paris and had even gone to the same elementary and high schools in Victoria. We were soon exchanging confidences and laughing merrily over the antics of art students and the peculiarities of professors. Emily

Emily Carr and Edythe Hembroff in Carr's studio on Simcoe Street (House of All Sorts), sketch by Edythe Hembroff-Schleicher from *Emily Carr: The Untold Story*

had learned to smoke in England many years before (which had scandalized her family) and I had acquired the habit in France, so we both lit a cigarette and settled back happily to reminiscences of student days.

As she warmed towards me Emily began to pour out her recollections. She told me about her childhood spent in the large Carr house on Government Street in Victoria, the happy

Emily Carr's birthplace, 207 Government St, Victoria, drawing by Edythe Hembroff-Schleicher

hours she shared with her sisters Lizzie and Alice, playing in the garden and surrounding fields. She described the sense of loss she felt as a young girl when first her mother and then her father died, and the resentment she felt towards her eldest sister who was left in charge of the younger Carr children. She said that she had been glad to escape from home at 18 to attend art school in San Francisco but that, once there, she realized art was much more to her than a means of escape; it was a way of life.

From that time on, Emily's course was set. When she returned to Victoria, six years later, she set up a studio in the loft above the cow barn on the family property, and began to teach. She made trips to the Indian villages on the coast, sketching the people and the totems. But she was thirsty for knowledge and as soon as she had saved sufficient funds she set off for England to continue her studies at the Westminster School of Art. She was totally unsophisticated and quite unequipped to face life in a big city like London. The five years she spent in England were overcast with illness, homesickness and a feeling of being cooped up. She was glad to get home, back to teaching in Vancouver and Victoria and to sketching once more among the Indians. She had felt that she would never leave Canada again.

Six years later, however, she went to Paris, this time to study the New Art which she felt might enable her to interpret the overwhelming vastness of the British Columbia landscape. Once more it was a time of exile, but Emily was satisfied that the experience was worth the effort; she felt better equipped to cope with the tremendous subjects waiting for her in British Columbia. She knew that her work was better—simpler in form, more direct in colour and more intense. It was all the more of a hurt, then, that at home her new style of painting met with scorn and ridicule. Her family was ashamed of her unconventional art and her unconventional ways: she smoked cigarettes, she came out with a good robust "damn" when it suited her, she rode astride, she surrounded herself with all kinds of animals, she wore convenient rather than fashionable clothes.

Emily admitted to me that she had become bitter at this reception. But she knew that she must hold fast to her own ideas. When people mocked, when she lost friends, when there were few pupils and no sales, she still refused to conform. She was convinced that she had found the right approach and she said she would rather starve than give in.

But how was she to earn a living? Inspiration came. Why not build a house with a number of suites and a studio for herself? She could live from the rental income and be free to paint as she wished. So she borrowed money and built the House of All Sorts on her share of the family land. Her dream, however, turned out to be a nightmare. The war came, rents fell, the cost of living rose, and Emily was forced to supplement her income by making pottery, hooking rugs, and raising English Bobtail sheepdogs. Worst of all, the tenants consumed all her time and strength; she had no energy left to devote to painting. For fifteen years her brushes lay idle.

Then, in 1927, came the turning point. Dr. Marius Barbeau, anthropologist at the National Museum in Ottawa, had heard of Emily through his interpreter at Port Simpson and had spoken of her to Eric Brown, Director of the National Gallery. Mr. Mortimer Lamb of Vancouver, long impressed with Emily's work, had also written to Mr. Brown on her behalf. On the strength of these recommendations, Eric Brown visited Emily's studio and invited her to send some of her paintings to Ottawa for an exhibition of Canadian West Coast Indian Art. Twenty-one of them were selected.

Provided with a railway pass, Emily went East to see the exhibition. On her way, she stopped off in Toronto and met the members of the Group of Seven. Emily told me that the inspiration provided by these men, in particular by Lawren Harris, gave her courage to go back to the woods again and try to capture their mystery on canvas. She had been painting ever since; her work was beginning to attract attention and she had even sold a few canvases. Only a month before, in March, she had held her first one-man show in the West, in the Crystal Garden in Victoria. It had been sponsored by the Victoria Women's Canadian Club, and Kathrene Pinkerton, an American writer then living in Victoria, had persuaded Emily to dress up for the occasion and even to give an address!

The big clock ticked on unnoticed until Emily suddenly jumped up, scattering protesting dogs in her hurry, and announced that it was cocoa time.

It was obvious to me even then that Emily Carr was a good teller of tales. Although she described much hardship, much bitter disappointment, there was a vein of humour in her anecdotes, she was always original in her viewpoint, and she was keenly observant of detail.

On this first visit, we didn't talk shop at all. The hours sped by too quickly for us to get around to any serious discussion of painting as such. She didn't even show me her work except to illustrate the story but while she was busy preparing our bread-and-butter-and-cocoa she allowed me to roam around and look at any stray canvases that were not stacked away. The animals came to life, anticipating the refreshment hour as a reward for their good behaviour. Woo pulled at her chain and jumped around impatiently before the fire. The dogs pattered around restlessly; Koko loyally attended his mistress in the kitchen, while Tinkle, my friend from the beginning, followed at my heels as I went from picture to picture. It was a memorable evening, the fore-runner of many pleasant, important evenings to be spent quietly in Emily's sanctum.

My family wanted me to stay at home for a while, so I turned a spare bedroom into a makeshift studio and started in to work on my fat portfolio of European sketches. My father made me a fine studio easel, which Emily envied, and bought me an etching press which she said was "an extravagance and a lot of nonsense." She did not like etchings. She considered etching a purely mechanical form of art not much above the level of china painting.

My friend, Marian Allardt, with whom I had studied in California and who had shared all my European experiences, came to visit me and we painted each other's portraits. The venture ended in disaster. As we were young and frivolous, we decided to pose in our best Paris evening gowns. I was very proud of mine; it was blue and filmy and awaiting its first wearing. After Marian had laid down her brushes at the end of a sitting, I backed slowly away from the canvas to get a better perspective. Absorbed in my inspection, I sat down on the edge of the couch. Alas!

Marian's painting materials had been carelessly laid down there and I sat right on her palette! Big daubs in all colours covered the seat of my lovely Paris creation and I was never able to wear it!

On my next visit to Emily, I told her about the catastrophe. She was unsympathetic, even gleeful. "That will teach you a lesson. You vain young things think only of appearances. You want to paint candy-box portraits and hash over old sketches when there is a wealth of solid, vital material right outside your front door and right in front of your unseeing eyes. I am disappointed in you. Is all your experience and training to be wasted? Are you a worker or just a pitiful painter like the old fogeys in the Arts and Crafts? Get your sketch book and work from nature which is the greatest teacher of all. André Lhote* called you "La Petite Sauvage" because you came from Canada. Well, show that you *are* from Canada and proud of it. Learn from the French, yes, but don't be hoodwinked by them."

This was the first of my many lectures. It left me shaken and a little bewildered. I had never liked landscape classes but only plunged enthusiastically into work when I had a nude, still-life or portrait to paint. I loved anatomy and even enjoyed studying the history of art which Emily dismissed in one word as "footle." I flourished in the studio atmosphere where Emily wilted and I became irritated with outdoor conditions—flimsy easel, bugs in paint, rapidly changing light and curious bystanders—which Emily somehow overlooked or overcame. But she had strength of mind and purpose and I was young and

*Famous French artist in whose atelier I studied for a year.

uncertain, and she managed to make me feel that one could not hope to be an artist if one remained indoors. Painting was sterile without ideas, she said. A suitable technique would develop as the idea grew but one must absorb one's environment like a sponge, and then interpret it fearlessly.

I protested at first, stood my ground and cited examples of great artists who had followed my path rather than hers, but she was firm in her resolve to win me from people to woods. My ultimate capitulation did me a great deal of harm, as my studies and paintings of forest subjects were always pale imitations of hers. Although I was to spend a great deal of time in the woods with her, I was never to feel them anything but cold, unapproachable, over-powering. I longed for warm, pulsating flesh again and often turned from the solemn trees to do sketches of Emily and the dogs, a cottage in the distance—anything which brought me in touch with everyday living again.

The summer passed, both of us painting hard. I took my landscapes and still-lifes to her for criticism and received valuable help. She even discussed her own work with me now, and once in a while I was allowed to see the "growing" canvases under the mysterious dust sheets. But she often treated me like a clumsy adolescent and never took my criticism seriously. She sat still, smoking a cigarette and stroking Koko, listening indulgently but with only half an ear. I discovered that she was not a good critic of her own work. She tended to have favourites which she especially liked because of some all-pervading idea which completely possessed her. This intensity was the secret of the power and the originality of her work but sometimes I felt that there were, from the point of view of composition, weak corners which could have been better organized to give unity to the whole. An artist, as he works, often develops a blind spot, and a fresh eye, even a relatively inexperienced one, can often be helpful. Emily always acknowledged her great debt to Lawren Harris for his sympathetic assistance and encouragement, and on a few occasions, she admitted receiving helpful "crits" from other artists, but on the whole, she remained indifferent and even antagonistic to opinion.

Indirectly, however, I was able to help her. She had few real friends in those days and Victoria was slow to recognize her as an artist. Her sisters continued to deplore her new approach to painting and she was constantly pressed for money. She therefore basked in my loyal friendship and sincere admiration for her fight to paint as her feelings dictated, uninfluenced by criticism or poverty.

One day Emily said to me, "Let's go out and paint a tree." I recognized this as propaganda, but agreed. We took two sketching stools, a few bits of paper and some charcoal (Emily loved charcoal as a medium) and wandered across Beacon Hill Park, past the white bear and the moth-eaten buffalo to the playing field beyond. Here we set up shop before a small stand of dark firs, just at the bend of a shaded road which curved out to the sea. An old gnarled veteran stood like a sentinel at the corner, spreading its branches before the background glade. "Draw *him*," commanded Emily. "I will watch and play the teacher today."

I could certainly draw a tree. I had taken a whole course in Tree Anatomy in San Francisco and shouldn't have been nervous. But I knew more was expected of me than just a good, accurate drawing. Even if the tree really seemed to grow, had properly articulated branches and was well co-ordinated to the background material, it still wouldn't be enough. I shifted my position so that she couldn't see my paper and settled down to

work. The stick of charcoal moved swiftly, in silence, for half an
hour. Then, dubiously, I presented the result.

"It's a good tree," she said at last, "but it's only the portrait of that tree. It does not express any universal feeling for *all* trees. It does not live among the other trees. It must breathe, have spirit! But it's a good start. You will learn more when we go into the woods together. There you will see only trees, think only trees and feel only trees."

My heart skipped a beat with pleasure, even though the "crit" was not very encouraging. She had always said she hated having people around when she was painting and now she was suggesting that I accompany her on a sketching trip! It meant that she had accepted me as a "worker" and not just as a "painter." She always drew a sharp line of distinction between the two terms. I felt both grateful and gratified.

Early in the fall, Emily phoned. "Look here," she said, "I am sending 'Poles in Early Skidigate' and 'Queen Charlotte Island Village' to the Northwest Artists' Show in Seattle. Crating's a nuisance but I do think that British Columbia artists should hold their end up. Why don't you send too?"

"Nothing good enough," I answered. "My work since I came home has just been groping around. You know how frightful it is."

"Some of it is good, solid stuff," she answered encouragingly. "I don't believe in showing old chestnuts but your Paris work still smells of fresh paint. Why not send over a couple of those?"

I followed her advice and, to everyone's astonishment, more particularly my own, one of my nudes was placed second in oils; I won fifty dollars, the Music and Art Foundation Prize.

Emily's first reaction was stunned amazement and I think her opinion of judges and exhibition procedure in general fell to an all-time low. On further consideration, however, she showed real pleasure in the award. She always championed my work stoutly and jealously when it was compared with that of other young Victoria artists, more especially that of Max Maynard and Jack Shadbolt whom, in spite of their promise, she regarded as "conceited young puppies." Jack had not entered a canvas in the show but I had been honoured over Max and other British Columbia artists and she openly gloated.

Another exhibitor from Victoria was Lodewyk Bosch, a young Dutchman who had come to the West Coast to write stories about Indians for "his public" in Holland, and who had stayed to show us Westerners how to paint. In Victoria, he felt near enough to the Orient to be influenced by its culture (nobody else did) and his flower studies took on a Japanesey flavour. He talked glibly about form, trends, and "isms" and Emily, who couldn't stand his affectations in speech or paint and called him "that Dutch turkey," boiled over with indignation. When Bosch visited her studio and announced that he discerned erotic symbolism in her work Emily gave him a look of withering scorn and curtly showed him the door.

As the fall blew into winter, we spent more and more evenings together before the studio fire. It was a cozy place to work and talk. Emily took four sticks of wood and four vises and made a frame so that I could start a hooked rug. I brought pants, dresses and all the odds and ends of wool garments I could find in the rag bag at home and hour after hour we plunged our needles in and out of the potato sack she had washed and stretched on the frames. Slowly the designs grew. Although I admired

Emily's bold Indian pattern, I did not copy her work. I felt it would be presumptuous of me to use an Indian motif without a little of her knowledge of Indian lore. After all, I had seldom seen an Indian other than the old women who used to sell their baskets from door to door when I was a child, and most of the totems I had seen were in the Metropolitan Museum of Art in New York. So I stuck to purely geometric forms.

Emily explained some of the Indian symbolism as she worked, and talked about the totem poles. She described her trips to Indian villages along the Skeena and Nass Rivers, on the Queen Charlotte Islands and on the stormy coast of Vancouver Island, and the unbelievable hardships they had entailed. She spoke with affection of her old friend Sophie who lived in the Indian village on the north shore of Burrard Inlet. She visited her often and always took along a cooked chicken and other treats. Sophie's village did not contain the massive and majestic totem poles that were to be found in more remote areas; her people were basket weavers, and many of Emily's wonderful baskets were valued gifts from Sophie or other Indian friends.

During these work evenings Emily also told me about her faithful friend Willie Newcombe, an expert in Indian lore, who was one of the few in Victoria who understood her and was always willing to help. He gave her advice about Indian matters and did most of her carpentry work, making frames, crates and racks for her pictures.

While we worked, the animals snoozed or enjoyed their own activities. Koko would lie full length on his side before the stove. Susie would snuggle up against him, and Woo would squat nearby, running quick, nervous fingers through the dog's shaggy hair. Occasionally she would find something, pop it into her mouth and work her jaws energetically.

"How can Koko have so many fleas?" I asked. Emily was insulted.

"He has no fleas," she snapped. "Woo is simply grooming Koko, looking for particles of salt from his skin which she likes to eat."

Tinkle usually watched this performance with curiosity, her tongue hanging out, not daring to intervene. My dog, Paris, who was restless in the studio, wandered around investigating, sometimes getting into trouble. Emily professed to love all animals but she really did not like Paris. When I accused her of this, she said that she never liked terriers as they were apt to be fickle. I felt, though, that it was unconfessed jealousy, like that of a mother who fears that attention may be detracted from her own brood. Paris was very smart, with his square clip, and was sometimes admired by casual passers-by on the street in preference to the griffons. This aroused all her protective maternal feeling and she often spoke sharply to Paris though his youthful sins were immeasurably fewer than those of the monkey who was the personification of mischief.

Whenever Woo got loose, she would make a bee-line for the kitchen where she would break all the eggs she could find. She would then skip back to the studio and scatter paint tubes everywhere; often she ate enough paint to make herself sick. Then she would systematically make a tour of the whole place, selecting small objects to stuff into her jowl pockets. And yet, in spite of the havoc she often caused, Woo was undoubtedly the favourite child.

Wherever Emily was, there her pets were also. She had had a passion for animals for as long as she could remember. As a child, though she had the companionship of Carlaw, the old family dog, and her pony Johnny, she had longed for a dog of her very own. It was a great event when, as a grown woman, she finally acquired Billie, the English Bobtail sheepdog which became the sire of her kennel and her constant companion. The sheepdogs were in time replaced by Belgian griffons but Emily was never again without a dog.

She had a magic touch with animals and seemed to be able to charm even the wild creatures. When she first returned to Victoria from San Francisco a handsome, strutting peacock from Beacon Hill Park called on her daily, courting her attention from the roof of her old cow barn studio. In England she raised wild song birds, and once she trained a big black raven to come into her kitchen for supper every night.

Usually her pets were well behaved; only Woo was consistently naughty. Emily admitted, though, that she had had a little trouble with her parrot once, when she tried to smuggle him across to Vancouver on the boat. She hid his cage under a blanket in her stateroom and was congratulating herself on the success of the plot when the parrot suddenly called out in his raucous voice, "God save George! God save George!"—to the utter consternation of the unknown woman in the lower berth. Emily said she wouldn't have minded so much if he'd said "God save the King" as he'd been taught; at least the woman would have known that he was a patriotic stowaway.

During the whole of that first winter, my visits to the studio continued regularly. I usually spent the work-talk evenings alone with Emily but occasionally other friends dropped in at the same time. Besides Willie Newcombe and Margaret Clay who were quite often there, I met Flora Hamilton Burns who, with Ruth Humphrey, was later to help Emily so much with her stories. Lizzie, the older sister, bustled in and out, and mild, devoted Alice, the favourite sister, sat silently, smiling rather sadly. Emily abused her sisters roundly at times but nevertheless had a real affection for them. Once after they had left together, she said to me rather wistfully, "I have been the tail of the family for so long it will be lonely for me when I am both head and tail."

Sometimes she allowed me to bring along a friend provided he wasn't English or a missionary. She was strongly prejudiced against Englishmen and missionaries and put it down to the fact that she had been over-exposed to their company when she was young. (Her oldest sister had surrounded herself with lah-di-dah English people who had aroused Emily's resentment, and Lizzie, who was very religious, had brought too many missionaries to the home.) Emily never recovered from these early impressions, never realized their basic unfairness. Though she had made few real friends during her student days in England, she generally regarded the English as sticky snobs and rarely gave an English person a chance to prove himself as an individual. She tended to "type" people and, once she had relegated a person to a category she did not like, she drew a shade over her critical faculties and refused to see good qualities—at least for a long time. She was often quick in temper, rash in judgment and called people "fools" with little provocation. Her classification was swift, all-inclusive and final.

One day, when something had gone awry with the water supply, she picked up the receiver. "I want the City Hall," she demanded of the operator. "City Hall? I want the Mayor. Is this the Mayor? This is Miss Emily Carr speaking. You are a great fool. The Town Council are all fools. The City Hall is packed with fools." Emily then hung up with vehemence in the middle of the Mayor's spluttering protests!

On one occasion, I took Lewis Rounding, my next-door neighbour, to meet her. He was a genial red-haired youth who was intrigued with my stories of the creatures and more anxious to see them than the paintings. After he had made a few polite but gauche remarks about her work, Emily took a wholehearted dislike to him, as she often did to young men, and sat grimly silent, stiff and unbending while I tried to breach the gap between them with casual conversation. My friend, feeling himself rebuffed, retreated to the warmer atmosphere of Woo's corner and started to play with her. Woo had been sewing. This was her favourite domestic activity. She loved to run a needle back and forth through a small scrap of flannel and would stamp her feet in anger if the needle had not been threaded. She looked completely absorbed, very innocent. But suddenly, annoyed at being disturbed in her work, she plunged her sharp little teeth into Lewis's caressing hand. I had always understood, rightly or wrongly, that monkey bites are dangerous and I was horrified. Lewis was also a bit shaken. Only Emily remained calm, insisting that her monkey was clean and couldn't hurt anyone. Even when she heard that Lewis had rushed to a doctor to get an injection of anti-tetanus she did not feel any compunction. "That fool shouldn't have teased her," was her comment. I always found Woo entertaining and enjoyed her but from that time on I kept a respectful distance if possible.

Now and again, I was privileged to meet callers from the East. Well-known Westerners had not, as yet, found the pathway to Emily's studio, but after 1927, when she held her first exhibition in Eastern Canada, various representatives of the Toronto world of art, letters or music came to see her. These were always red-letter days for Emily who was starved for sympathy, appreciation and contact with serious artists. She talked about such a visit for days before and days afterwards and was as excited as a young girl going to her first ball.

I remember Mr. and Mrs. Adaskin's visit, particularly. They wanted to see the van that Emily had bought for her sketching trips, so I drove them out to Metchosin where it sat in a field wintering—empty, solitary. Mr. McCurry, later Director of the National Gallery, dropped in to see Emily while I was there and I talked to him briefly. Members of the Hart House Quartet remembered her and their visits gave her deep pleasure.

I recollect that on one occasion I was invited to help entertain Dr. and Mrs. Lismer who were coming to supper. This was another "party" entailing the usual excitement of anticipation and preparation and I was caught up in the flurry. I did the shopping and then, having chained Woo securely and put the dogs into the garden, we retired to the kitchen to get a start on the *pièce de résistance*, a curry. Emily always prided herself on her cooking. Not everybody enjoyed it, as it was inevitably associated with dogs, monk and Susie, but she could make an excellent "mess of curry" and a few other house specialities when she was primed with the party spirit.

The Lismers came. Dr. Lismer said a great deal and Mrs. Lismer very little but the evening, I thought, went off very pleasantly with much picture talk and a good meal. Dr. Lismer looked at canvas after canvas. He praised, criticized and joked. I was impressed by his profound knowledge of art, his quick eye for the good or bad in a painting and his amusing informality. Emily was graciousness itself. She joined in the fun and seemed to appreciate Dr. Lismer's comments. But after they were gone she broke out into a wail! "I am so confused! I *know* he didn't like my work. He doesn't take it seriously at all! And Mrs. Lismer didn't eat my curry! The evening was a flop!"

*T*he gray winter skies of Victoria gave way to the blue of spring and, as Emily watched the trees acquire a shimmering halo of green and the purple heads of crocuses pop through the soil, she grew restless. Early spring was always her favourite time in the woods, and she was eager to pick up her sketching paraphernalia and run. The forest bursting into new life was an ever-recurrent theme in her work. She particularly liked to be in the woods when the contrast in colour and movement between the old and young growth was greatest and the woods gayest. The work she did at these periods is permeated with an exuberant feeling of spring. At this time of year, too, she had a driving urge to leave the terrible tenants and their woes behind, to turn her back on the insatiable furnace and to live quietly on a flat stretch of land after the miles of stairs she had climbed all winter.

The time had come to make good the promise she had made to me in Beacon Hill Park.

"Where shall we go and how soon can we start?"

We discussed ways and means. The means were, as usual, a determining factor. Although she had exhibited widely since 1927 and the National Gallery had purchased three of her pictures, sales had continued to be slow. Sometimes she sold sketches to friends or callers for a mere pittance just because five or ten dollars were badly needed. We therefore decided on Cordova Bay because of the free roof provided by my family's summer cottage there. Studio and kitchen hummed with preparation. Complete supplies for eating, sleeping and painting had to be assembled and somehow stacked in or on the car. We looked like a one-car circus as we finally drove off—excited animals stirring about on the heaped-up contents inside; easels, bed rolls and valises tied, strapped or dangling outside.

The camp was situated half way between beach and road on a steep piece of heavily wooded property. The lush undergrowth, which threatened to submerge the cottage during its fall and winter seclusion, was cleared out each spring, leaving dank, moist soil between the hemlocks which then produced a luxuriant crop of skunk-cabbages with wan, yellow flowers. From the front verandah, overlooking the tops of spirea bushes, there was a magnificent view of the straits. In the foreground was a sweep of fine beach, its white sand piled high with large logs that had been thrown up by the winter waves.

The still waters of Georgia Strait were rolling back from the beach as we arrived, uncovering the immense rippled sandbar where we sometimes dug for clams and where we took the dogs for their daily frolic. When the tide was high, Seal Rock, in the middle foreground, where seals came to sun themselves, was scarcely visible. But now, with the sandbar fully exposed, it could be reached on foot, over flesh-rending barnacles, through a narrow channel of sand-warmed water. Beyond was Leper Island and, on the horizon, the long strip of San Juan over which, on clear days, could be seen the magnificent colourful cone of Mount Baker.

The first day was spent in settling in. The camp was crude but comfortable. In fact, Emily, accustomed to still cruder and very cramped sketching quarters, complained about the luxury and space. We and the dogs rattled around, she said, "like peas in an over-large pod." Emily, who really seemed to enjoy obstacles in everyday living because it gave scope to her amazing ingenuity, was confronted with no problems to solve here. Firewood neatly piled by the back door lay ready for use. There were plenty of solid tables and chairs, a sink with running water and a bedroom apiece with spares for the dogs. The stove, usually her bugbear, functioned perfectly. Living was so simple, so smooth, that we had most of the day free for real work.

The next morning we made our first trip into the woods. Weighted down with our sketching materials, Woo skipping along on her chain attached to Emily's waist, Paris, Koko and the other dogs bringing up the rear, we tramped along the hot, tarred road to "Little Arctic," the store and social centre, then up a shaded grade, across the railroad to the woods. We did many sketches there but Emily was disappointed in the material. The woods were not deep enough, not remote enough. The straggling colony of summer cottages seemed to invade and civilize at every turn, even though they were largely unoccupied. Because this was Emily's first attempt to interpret seashore material intensively I think that no really important work resulted from our stay at Cordova Bay. But she did absorb impressions from the scene around her and come to grips with her subject, thus getting what she called "much good study." She profited from this later on in her studio when she reworked the many beach and log sketches that were the products of this trip. One fine canvas, "Cordova Drift," a composition made up of elements from several of the paper studies, was first shown in the library of the University of British Columbia in November 1938.

On rainy days Emily sometimes worked from the verandah, painting the shore-line and logs or else the panorama before her. But she really did not love the sea as she loved the woods and her seascapes are therefore relatively few and not always convincing.

Emily did love the mountains, though, and she often deplored the lack of surrounding mountains in Victoria; she felt that the beautiful Olympics on the horizon were too distant, cold and remote. She longed to paint *real* mountains, to be right in them, to get at their core, to interpret their weight and mass. Later she achieved this ambition when she found an opportunity to paint in the Lillooet. From there she wrote a letter which made a profound impression on me. She was painting a mountain for the first time and was experiencing discouraging difficulty in conveying her feeling of the inner bulk-weight of her subject. In her despair, she said she envied the miners who daily went to and fro because they could hack at the mountain-side and so learn precisely the nature of "her" substance. (Emily often spoke of her subjects as animate beings—and if they were "difficult" they were, for some reason, always feminine.) This mountain, in particular, became a real *bête noire* to her, a stubborn, unyielding monster reluctant to see its splendid, powerful mass harnessed on paper. She fought with it day after day until it collapsed and "died." She resurrected it again and again but it was a long time before she felt she had really conquered it.

Though there was no very provocative material at Cordova Bay, this first sketching trip together was memorable for one thing: it proved that Emily could work and live in harmony with another person. She had thought this impossible and had made the suggestion that I accompany her with many misgivings. Although she "hated having people about," we had only one quarrel, just one quick flash of anger over the trifling matter of where the teaspoons should be kept. Perhaps she found me too passive and rural life with no "ructions" a little monotonous. In that case, a teaspoon would be as good a pretext as any for giving vent to her stored-up feelings.

The last day came inevitably. We regretfully started our packing. Woo was sitting on her favourite perch, atop a partition which divided the sitting room from the spare bedroom, alertly watching proceedings. Clothes and painting materials were scattered in confusion over tables, chairs and floor. Emily plucked out her "town" shoes from a pile of clothing and set them down in readiness against the partition wall. When the time came to go she sat down to put on her shoes. She put in one foot—splosh! "Damn!" she said roundly and gazed for a moment, stunned, at her damp stocking. Then she looked at Woo and realization dawned. She grabbed the monkey roughly and gave her the spanking of her life. Even Emily Carr could not house-break a monkey!

Emily detested dates. In school she could never recall the years of major events, and in her own life she said that the only one she could recall was her "born" date. This airy attitude to the calendar causes me difficulties now, as she often didn't bother to date a picture and her letters rarely bear any other designation than the day of the week. But there is one advantage: she would hardly expect *me* to be punctilious about these matters and I need not therefore apologize for the fact that I cannot with certainty say just when we went on our second sketching trip. It was, I think, the following fall, in September 1931.

This time we went to the Goldstream Flats. Conditions were entirely reversed on this expedition. Sketching material was infinitely better than at Cordova but we paid dearly for the improvement, in the primitive living arrangements. It was not easy to find inexpensive accommodation for two or three weeks' duration only. We combed the countryside, questioned passers-by, knocked at doors and called at stores. Finally, a depressing little structure was offered us. Unpainted, carelessly thrown together on a small bald spot flush with the highway, its only attractive feature was the price: $5 a month. It was a converted garage and the only things which elevated it from its original status were one small window and a doubtful stove. We brought two cots, a table, basins, jugs and pails to substitute for plumbing, packed food and sketching materials, rounded up the dogs, squeezed in, and called it home.

The shanty had the further disadvantage of being quite far from the Flats so we had long, loaded hikes back and forth each day. Paris was the only one who enjoyed these tramps. The griffons, with their short, unexercised legs, panted and puffed, barely making the finishing line, and Woo pulled on her chain, scolding, trying to tell Emily she had had enough.

In our close quarters, all was a temper-trying huddle of beasts, possessions, artists. We stepped over dogs and on dogs and got in one another's way constantly in the simple process of cooking or undressing. The matter of sponge bathing and getting dressed and undressed modestly was a real problem in our one small room. I stripped shamelessly while Emily averted her eyes but she was of a different era. Her family had been early Victorian, easily scandalized, never admitting that a nude body filled out the decent drapes which covered it. Although she had worked in life classes in San Francisco and London, her early prudish education was too ingrained to overcome intellectually and she always made a clear-cut distinction between a nude in class and a naked body in everyday life. Her excessive modesty was a torment even to herself at times. It seemed affected and even embarrassing to me but I tried to reduce the fuss to a minimum by co-operating with her various systems for remaining invisible. For the bath and in the mornings, I was simply put out-of-doors like one of the dogs but at night this seemed impracticable. At first she tried undressing under her nightgown but no amount of wiggling could shed the undergarments without undue effort. I was therefore put on the "honour system" to gaze straight ahead at a spot on a chosen wall until the operation was concluded.

In spite of the trials of daily routine which we soon learned to make light of, we had a wonderfully happy time together. As far as work was concerned, this trip, I think, was the most successful. A large number of good sketches resulted and a few important canvases. We both loved the Flats. We felt that we had been transported hundreds of miles away on a magic carpet each time we went into the cool, serene glade of imposing, straight cedars. They were more reminiscent of the great redwood stands in California than the woods which otherwise encircle Victoria. Summer picnickers had gone and an enveloping silence remained. There was no tangled undergrowth to break the soaring lines of the great tree boles which rose majestically from a floor of soft, delicate moss. Hanging fronds gave them the appearance of old bearded men. In colour, line and mood, it was a new and exciting material and, for the first time, I felt I was getting my teeth into a forest subject and did a few sketches which Emily said were quite good.

She sat quietly on her little camp stool for the greater part of the first day, absorbing, thinking, and jotting down notes. But then the sketches followed in rapid succession. Once she had her focal point and her idea, her brush always moved rapidly with hardly a pause. There was one rule which had to be obeyed. I was never to disturb her while she was thinking. She chatted while she painted but when she slowly extracted a home-made cigarette from the battered tin box she always carried with her and just sat before her subject, I knew this was a signal for silence.

We had our fun too. Relaxation came at noon when we woke up the dogs and roamed down to the little brook to eat the box lunch we had brought with us. I would wander into the clear, cold water and play with Paris while Emily took Woo and the dogs for a short walk, or just lay on her back on the bank of the brook listening to the birds and answering their calls. Sometimes she would reread a few passages from her well-worn copy of Walt Whitman's *Leaves of Grass*.

Emily was to sketch at the Flats again, two years later, just after she bought her van, but the satisfying experience of the first trip was not repeated. She complained of gravel and wood trucks driving in and out, mutilating and destroying roads, peace and growth. The very strangeness of this spot which had so appealed to us seemed incongruous to her later. "The immense trees are of a different time and place to the other stuff," she said. "There is no second growth to fill the gap."

Even today I think back on those two and a half weeks with much pleasure and I realize more and more what a privilege it was to work so intimately with her in the field.

Back in town, Emily plunged into an orgy of work. She did not often retouch field sketches, preferring to start afresh if she felt some particular idea merited further study. Some of the sketches she developed into canvases but the canvas was never a copy of the original piece. At times the changes were superficial, as in her large painting of a single cedar bole, but at other times the idea caught in the sketch was used as a starting point only and the canvas, as it grew, took on new form and meaning. Occasionally she combined two or even three sketches to make a composite picture. Although she usually sketched in oils, her paintings had an entirely different character when she worked on canvas. It was as if she used a different medium. In the field, she used gasoline freely in mixing her pigments so that her light, flowing lines had almost the transparency of watercolours. (Indeed, many people thought they *were* watercolours. Even Mr. Brown, former Director of the National Gallery, could be fooled on this score. In 1939, when the gallery was considering the purchase of two canvases, he wrote Emily complimenting her on her "water-colour Sky." This was, of course, one of her oil sketches.) Her sketches had spontaneity and gaiety. The paper itself played a part, as patches of it were left uncovered. In her canvases, she used a heavier pigment, usually darker in colour, and they were more laboured, more consciously organized. At one period, her forest growth was worked into drape-like folds, almost cubistic in pattern.

She was often depressed about her work, often felt that

it was mediocre, and her despair boiled over into letters to Lawren Harris, who wrote her helpful and encouraging advice in return. Sometimes she would read me parts of these letters before the fire in the evening and I realized what strength and comfort she drew from them. Later on, she was to feel that she and Lawren were travelling different roads, was to find him too theoretical, too engrossed in the abstract to derive the same relief and "working help" from the correspondence. But for many years she was very dependent on him for guidance.

The only event to break the even tenor of the fall days was the annual exhibition by the local Island Arts and Crafts Society. Emily contributed to these shows spasmodically, depending on whether her sense of duty or feeling of disgust got the upper hand. The Society was always a thorn in Emily's flesh and a constant state of war existed between her and the group. She had a broad, universal outlook on art which conflicted with that of the good souls of the Society who tried ineffectively to keep the feeble spark of art in Victoria flickering with pretty pictures which had no relation to art as Emily saw it. She hated giving even tacit approval to these little "social" exhibitions by offering her work, but then would be influenced by the fact that any art group was probably better than none. The members of the society, for their part, were disturbed and shocked by Emily's paintings. As her work gained recognition, however, and she was praised far afield, it was undeniably an honour to have her participate. And so, at last, a sort of truce was established.

My work, however, did not have the merit of being well known and the canvas I proposed to submit that fall had the disadvantage of being a nude, or worse, a group of nudes. I had been reading Thomas Mann's *The Magic Mountain*, in one part of which he describes the female body as a series of triangles. The idea interested me and I used it as a theme for a large canvas. There were several nudes composed of a multitude of triangles. The picture was therefore shocking on two scores: it was naked and it was cubistic. Of course, I might have conformed to tradition and submitted a landscape but Emily, out of pure devilment, insisted on the triangles. We sent in our respective pictures and then sat back to wait for the fun. It came. Apparently the old ladies were puffed up with indignation and the feathers flew. Emily was consulted and she said her canvases would be withdrawn if mine was refused. And so, under threat, I "made" the Arts and Crafts show. We visited the gallery and Emily insisted on standing near the nudes to get the full benefit of remarks for future savouring. She chuckled all the way home. I had rarely seen her so amused.

This was my last showing with the Island Arts and Crafts proper but later, when Max Maynard was Vice-President of the Society, he persuaded the committee to an act of boldness. Under the Society's auspices, an exhibition of the work of Emily Carr (seven pictures), Max, Jack Shadbolt and myself was held in the Belmont Building on Government Street. Max wrote an introductory note, printed in the catalogue, telling fellow-citizens about "modem" art. The show made quite a splash. It was a success. Some scoffed, but many were interested.

The Arts and Crafts affair over, an intensive sewing-bee began. Emily had bought a machine on the instalment plan (how hard it was for her to make the payments later!) and about once a year she ran up a whole supply of garments for herself and a fresh wardrobe for Woo made from scraps. It went quickly because everything, dresses, slips and nightgowns, was from the same pattern. No bias cut, no ruffles, yokes, gores or pleats. In dressmaking and housekeeping, as well as in painting, she had much of the pioneer spirit inherited from her father. She found a way of making, fixing or simplifying almost every-thing. Appearance was never a concern. If it worked it was satisfactory. To save money, she tackled plumbing, carpentry and stove repairs. She sized and stretched her own canvases and made her own easels. She once made a cot out of an old moosehide, and even made her own soap. In these small, daily matters, she was more ingenious than anyone I have ever met. She was practically self-sufficient.

*I*n late November 1932 the first of my long absences from Victoria began. Our constant companionship suffered its first break and our correspondence started. Unfortunately, I did not think then of keeping her letters so that those I have preserved are from a much later date. I regretted leaving Victoria although the prospect of spending the winter in Santa Barbara with my sister Helen Hembroff was appealing. California was my second home.

The winter passed quickly. It seemed only a matter of days until I was back in Emily's studio again. She had had a good winter of work but her old grievances had not lessened. There were still few friends, few dollars and slow acclaim. Almost her first question was: "When do we go to camp?" The call of the spring woods was strong again and Emily was eager to leave.

"Let's call on Mrs. McVicker," she said. "She has some kind

of a hunting lodge in the Sooke hills which she might let us have."

Mrs. McVicker was an old friend of Emily's. She had at one time had a small antique shop in Victoria and now had a few pigs and sheep in the country. It was from Mrs. McVicker's sheep that Emily got the raw wool to make the lovely set of three creamy-coloured hooked rugs which, the following winter, was to bring her a little much-needed income. Mrs. Mac was at home, a hearty woman both in physique and speech. Of course we could have the lodge. She gave us the key and we moved in the next week.

The cabin was a delight. Gray with years, tumble-down, it had the advantage of being completely isolated. I had difficulty getting the car through the bumpy, overgrown trail which led to our sunny clearing, dotted with dark tree stumps. All around were lonely woods, so unaccustomed to human activity that deer often nosed their way curiously into our back yard. The cabin consisted of one large all-purpose room with a stone fireplace and a little newspaper-lined kitchen which leaned crookedly against the sitting room for support. The main room had character. It even had a semblance of interior decoration. Curtains hung at the windows—limp curtains, it is true, but the faded pattern still was bright enough to be cheerful. The most outstanding feature of the room, however, was a ledge which completely encircled it and on which, lined up like soldiers, was a solid line of steins! A whole regiment of steins! Steins of every conceivable shape, size and material. Dignified steins, comic steins! Perhaps this was all that was left of Mrs. McVicker's antique shop.

After our first delighted inspection, we turned to essentials. There was no wood; we would have to get what we needed from the forest. There was no W.C.; we had to make one. Worse still, there was, practically speaking, no stove. The rusty heap of iron in the kitchen which looked like a stove refused to behave like one, even with Emily's expert coaching and coaxing. She patched, petted and poked but, finally, despite years of experience with stubborn stoves, she had to admit defeat. With parts of the monster she made a stove of sorts in the fireplace and on this we did all our cooking. By arrangement, she was the cook and I the wood-chopper and I think her back ached as much as mine as she bent over the low grate. But we had good meals. She even succeeded in making tea-biscuits in a frying pan!

Emily had developed a new sketching technique which, evolved for purely practical reasons, formed the basis for a completely different approach to her work. She was faced by the need to economize; she couldn't keep up her usual scale of productivity without cutting down on expense somewhere. White paint and paper made the biggest dent in her pocket-book so she experimented with tins of ordinary white house paint of a good quality and bought large sheets of cheap Manila paper in wholesale quantities. The Manila paper, besides being cheap, had two added advantages: it provided a larger painting surface on which she could interpret more freely her woods subjects, and it gave her sketches of a standardized size, which simplified exhibiting and framing. From then on, she used only this large-size Manila paper in the field and to transport it she made a folding drawing board which was easy to carry. In time she produced a large collection of these paper sketches uniform in size and technique.

In those days, Emily was at the height of her productive powers. The number of sketches she brought home from this and later trips was impressive. Routinely, unless weather interfered, she did three a day. We got up about seven but by the time we had hauled water, chopped wood, got the fire going and fed ourselves and the creatures, a good chunk of the morning had slipped away and it was usually ten before we had found our subject and started to paint. We worked again from two to four and later returned to the woods for an early evening sketch. After a rather late supper, we always held our private exhibition. We tacked the day's work on the walls and discussed it. I was often discouraged after Emily's "crits" and took mine down and kicked them under the bed in disgust but she left hers up all night. She loved to lie in bed in the morning and study them with a fresh eye in the bright light.

Mrs. Mac came to see us one day. She was our first and only visitor on this trip so it was an event worthy to be called a "party." It was a primitive party but we put our best cooking foot forward and even found something we could call a tablecloth. That night, a deer must have come close, unseen and unheard, because the next day we had our second guests—deer ticks! Tinkle and I were the unfortunate victims. One burrowed into my breast and the other into Tinkle's mouth. Nothing would dislodge these blood-sucking torments. I had never even heard of a deer tick before and now I was harbouring one, festering and itching. Poor Tinkle sat woefully slobbering, slobbering, trying to scratch away her parasite. On the following day, however, Emily had an inspiration. She had heard that deer ticks don't like gasoline and that they would back out on application. We ran for her paint box, dabbed on the gasoline. Sure enough! The little wretches beat a hasty retreat.

After sketching for the year was over and we were working in the studio again, I said to Emily, "I am always doing what you like to do. I have painted at least a thousand trees. Why shouldn't we do a still life or a portrait for a change? It is just possible that a new subject might give you stimulating study. Everybody needs a holiday."

She was dubious. It was hard for her to step out of her woods but she agreed in the end, rather reluctantly. She cleared a corner for me by the big window and allowed me the use of one of her easels. We set up a still life and she grudgingly admitted that she enjoyed the work. "No green in the drapes," she had ordered. "If this is to be a holiday, I want big splashes of bright colours." Encouraged by this enthusiasm, I next suggested a model. Alice offered one of the little boys from her school and he was coaxed to sit quietly by promises of a walk with the monkey and a movie. We did two studies of this child, one with a big apple in his hands and the other, because the apple tended to disappear during rest periods, without the apple. Emily worked on paper and I think didn't keep the sketches. Mine was on canvas and was always my mother's favourite painting. Later it at least paid its way as it won first prize for oils at the Victoria exhibition.

My next proposal was for an exchange of portraits. We sat for one another. Hers was again on paper, her usual Manila size. She painted me in soft colours, yellows and blues. The dress had stripes of these colours and even the face contained a lot of grayed blues and yellows. She did not strive for a realistic likeness but, in a few deft, quick strokes, she nevertheless did a portrait which was undeniably me. She had had fun with the still life but she quickly became bored with the portraits. Essentially she did not like people; nothing in them compelled her interest sufficiently to make her want to express their qualities, good or bad, in paint. By the time she got to me, she was impatient to finish off a bad bargain and, as she worked, she occasionally burst into song:

Oh! would that you were a tree-ee-ee,

Oh! would that you were a tree.

When it came time for me to paint her portrait I was surprised to discover that even Emily Carr had her vain moments: she dressed up for the portrait I was to do of her. She put on her best black dress, a little bolero jacket and even pinned a cameo brooch at her throat. She sat still as a rock, determined to do her duty, and I teased her by saying that she could have made a better living as a model than as an artist.

I don't know whether she liked the portrait when it was finished. Probably not. She perhaps told others that "it gave her the pip," which is the way she described the only other portrait done of her, from life, in her later years—an interesting and capable portrait by Nan Cheney. Emily considered Nan's portrait to be too much of a caricature and she didn't like the background. It nevertheless won praise in exhibitions and was sold, I believe, in the East.

My painting portrayed Emily faithfully enough but it was unexciting, unimaginative. I did not really like it. Therefore, when I left Vancouver some years later, it suffered the same fate as forty-eight other canvases, including Emily's portrait of me: it was torn up and thrown into the garbage can. I thought that was the end of the portrait episode but instead, it turned out to be the beginning of a strange story. Years later, in Ottawa, in 1949, I heard indirectly that the Vancouver Art Gallery was in possession of a portrait of Emily by an unknown artist. According to the rumour, the picture had been found, slashed, in a garbage tin, had somehow found its way to the gallery and there had been restored, as though it were an old master, by an expert, Mr. Tyler. I wrote to the gallery describing my painting and received the confirmation that it was indeed mine!

Emily Carr at Metchosin, sketch by Edythe Hembroff-Schleicher from *Emily Carr: The Untold Story*

The 1932 trip to the Sooke hills was to be my last sketching trip with Emily. The next year she bought a van and although I often spent full days working with her while she was parked at Albert Head near Victoria, I could not possibly have telescoped myself into the van to sleep. Emily equipped the "Elephant," as she called it, with a bed, an oil stove, shelves, and special nooks for the animals, and had it towed to various "woodsey" spots over a period of years. In it she led the gypsy-like life so dear to her heart and found the solitude she craved for painting and study and, later, for intensive writing. To honour the purchase of the van she even named one of her new puppies Caravana.

On her first sketching trip in the Elephant, Emily had the company of Henry Brand as well as her animals. Henry, who lived with his sister in the apartment next to Emily's studio, was mentally retarded as a result of childhood encephalitis. He was as nervous and jittery as an aspen leaf but had a childlike affection and trust for those he liked. He hopped, stuttered and wriggled his way into the hearts of all who knew him. Henry enjoyed country life and took pride in doing little chores. He liked taking care of the animals and they responded to him. After two weeks of fresh air and Emily's camp-style cooking he went home feeling better and brighter.

As it happened Henry was a friend of mine as well. I had met him and his brother Frederick, whom I was later to marry, in 1930. Max Maynard brought us together. Max had been an old class-mate of mine at Victoria High School and he had called on me on my return from Paris because he was interested in painting. He invited my sister and me to "Innisfree," the Maynard hide-away on the edge of a deserted, burned-out logging camp near Cowichan. Here we were introduced, first, to Henry Brand and Angelina, the goat.

"What in the world are you doing in such a desolate spot?" I asked Max.

"It's quite simple," he replied. "The clover that has grown over the charred countryside is ideal for honey. My father has set up an apiary here and Henry is helping him to tend the bees and look after Angelina. Frederick, Henry's brother, is here too. He has just returned from two years at Oxford and wants a remote, quiet place to read philosophy. I am painting, and Angelina provides food and entertainment."

Frederick, hearing our voices, now emerged from a hut. He had unruly curly hair and large thoughtful gray eyes. Only the summer beard helped him to look mature enough to be what he was, an Assistant Professor of Mathematics at the University of British Columbia. The awesome subject of mathematics and his aloof bearing disconcerted me at first, but we soon found a common interest: Emily Carr. Frederick had read widely on art and had gained an appreciation of the modern trend in painting while overseas. He was amazed, he said, to find such an advanced exponent of the creative movement as Emily Carr right at home.

Frederick described his first meeting with Emily. Max had introduced them the year before. He had rushed home one day to say that a Canadian genius was living near the Park, a woman who painted Indian things. He arranged to visit her studio and took Frederick along.

Frederick's first impressions were somewhat similar to mine. On the whole, though, he sensed more suspicion in her greeting than I did, less frankness and warmth. He did not know then that this was always her reaction to the visit of young men to her studio. On that particular day her manner was stiff; she showed her canvases grudgingly, as though the integrity of her art were threatened, and she remained aloof during the whole "interview." She seemed in no hurry to accept the professions of two bright young men but was nonetheless pleased, he thought, to hear her pictures called good, indeed, wonderful. She melted a little.

"There are so few who think my pictures good," she said, "and fewer still who say so. The public is uninformed, vague, and only articulate when it condemns."

"But, what about the juries at exhibitions?" Frederick asked. "They should know better. They are the experts and have the fatal authority, and yet they have banished you too and rejected your work."

"Those blind idiots!" Emily exclaimed. "They have hung up

on the walls all the birds' nests, and pretty little broom picture post cards, and gawky Highland cows—and left me on the floor, in a corner. That's where I found my things, getting spattered with dish-water in the kitchen!"

From the moment of this first encounter with Emily, Frederick was one of her keenest admirers and never missed an opportunity to further her career. He came to know her quite well as a person when he was living with his sister one summer in the House of All Sorts, preparing for a year in the Graduate College, Princeton. He took over Emily's dining-room as a study and the attic loft up the winding staircase, where eagles' wings spread over the rafters and shingles of the ceiling, as his bedroom.

They quarrelled the first day, over the use of the bathroom which was plastered with notices generously spattered with exclamation marks: "Don't throw matches in the toilet!" "Don't use Draino!" "Rinse out basin!" And, over the bathtub: "Don't splash!"

Frederick obeyed these orders meticulously, but Emily had other complaints. He took too long to shave, and shouldn't have a beard anyway. Above all, though, he certainly had no business being in view in the hall when she wanted to go to the bathroom. There was a thumping, high-voiced row followed by the slam of Emily's door. Frederick almost packed up and moved out.

But the next day was extraordinarily calm and still. Even the dogs were quiet. Emily had had second thoughts and had organized a new routine. All went smoothly throughout the remainder of his stay and there were no more scenes.

She and Frederick often had lunch together on the verandah, simple, nourishing lunches with salad, brown bread, cheese or cold meat, fruit and tea. She had a good appetite and enjoyed food. Meals with her were pleasant because she both chatted and listened. They discussed all manner of subjects, from the works of D. H. Lawrence to Emily's impression of an Indian potlatch she had once attended.

It was Frederick who introduced Emily's work to the University of British Columbia. In March 1933, he organized an exhibition of her paintings in the Library there and included canvases by Max Maynard and myself to give variety to the show. Cartage costs were paid by a few members of the Faculty. The letters of invitation which Frederick sent to the Faculty, Senate and Board of Governors stated: "Miss Carr's art ranks among the most vigorous, individual, and creative work that is being done on this continent today." He gave a talk on her paintings in the Library at the opening of the exhibit which excited lively comment among the students. Press notices were good and many visitors from the city came out to see the show. Opinion was by no means all favourable but the reaction was definite and spirited in the modern as well as the conservative camp and this led to stimulating discussions. Frederick acted as guide to the students and defended Emily's canvases in an article, "Great Art Hidden In Kitchens" in the campus paper, *The Ubyssey*. As a result of this little storm interest in her work grew. Two of the professors, Dr. G. G. Sedgewick and Hunter Lewis, became immediate converts. Dr. Sedgewick bought a Lillooet sketch and later assisted Emily with her writing. Hunter also bought a sketch and began to write and lecture about her life and work.

In that same year, 1933, Emily was honoured by another Victoria club, of which she was a member. A committee of three called at Emily's studio and selected "Vanquished," a painting of a deserted Indian village in the Queen Charlotte Islands, to send to the International Fine Arts Exhibition in Amsterdam. That strong, stark canvas had the spiritual quality common to all Emily's mature work, and was well reviewed by the critics. She was much "bucked up" by the reception it received.

*I*t was in the spring following our last sketching trip together that an ambition began to take root in Emily's mind. She wanted to visit the World's Fair in Chicago to see the picture exhibition. She was selling more frequently now but at ridiculously low prices and there was still no room for extras in her budget, particularly for an item as large as a train ticket East. She still cursed her sewing machine payments and had taken out burial insurance so that she would not be a burden on her sisters in case of death. She knew the whole idea of the trip was impracticable but it teased her constantly. She could not give it up.

I lay in bed one night, sleepless, trying to think out a plan which would make the trip possible. Suddenly, I hit on a scheme. "Emily," I said the following day, "I think it can be managed. If you will let me have one of your paintings, I will try to convince friends and clubs that it should be presented to the British Columbia Government on a donation basis."

Emily hesitated. "It looks too much like charity," she said, "to beg for money. I would be ashamed."

"Nonsense," I retorted. "It is shocking that the British Columbia Archives have never purchased one of your Indian canvases. It is therefore the duty of public-spirited citizens to provide them with one."

It was not actually very difficult to override her objections; her desire to go was too strong. We considered a number of totem paintings and decided on "Kispiox Totems," a large canvas.

I started my campaign. Several Victoria women's clubs responded liberally to my appeal and their support gave me a good solid foundation on which to solicit small contributions from friends and well-wishers. Slowly, slowly the fund grew and, with the assistance of another friend of Emily's, Mrs. Anstie, I ultimately got enough ($166) to make Chicago a certainty.

The canvas was duly presented to the Archives, in a small ceremony in the Parliament Buildings. Frederick made a short speech of presentation and a few words of acceptance were spoken by a representative of the Provincial Premier. Emily was so delighted when she received the proceeds of the canvas that she gave me my first picture as a token of appreciation. She chose it purely because of the title: "Joy."

Her trip was to be, in one sense, a deep disappointment.

She left Victoria too late and found on arriving in Chicago, that the exhibition had been closed on her very nose—as she put it—twelve hours before arrival. It was a bitter pill to swallow. She methodically went through the gestures of visiting the Fair proper but it did not impress her greatly and her heart was not in it. After six days she became terribly homesick. Then she had a thought which saved the whole trip and made everything worthwhile. Why not go to Toronto and at least see pictures there and talk to her many good friends? She stayed with Mrs. Housser who invited about forty people, mostly artists, to tea in her honour. She was given a wonderful welcome. The greatest thrill of all, however, was the "joyful thing" she took home with her—one of Lawren Harris's Arctic sketches!

Even before Emily left for the East I was off in the same direction, to work at commercial art in New York with my California friend Marian and to study in my spare time. There was quite a group of Victorians in New York that year; Connie Ross Ohrt, Jack Shadbolt and John MacDonald had congregated there too, and we did full justice to the city's nightspots and restaurants as well as to its museums and concert halls. When we returned to the West Coast, Emily gave a large party for us in her studio. My sister Ruth, back in Victoria to show mother and father their first grandchild, was a wide-eyed guest. Jack had picked up a little surrealism in New York and pontificated on his latest theory. It was a pleasant evening of talk, everyone seemed to have been doing and seeing a great deal, and Emily was never such an agreeable hostess.

Frederick Brand and I had been married in New York and Emily gave us a seascape, "Off Dallas Road," for a wedding present. But this did not satisfy us. We wanted a large, important canvas too. We looked longingly at several favourites every time we went to her studio but even at her sharply reduced "wholesale" prices they were too expensive for us at the time. When, however, "Blunden Harbour" was finished, I could hold out no longer.

"That is the one we want," I said. "Will you sell it to us on the instalment plan?"

She reminded me of her payments on the sewing machine and said she did not want to inflict this type of torture on us.

"At least," I temporized, "will you give us the option on it? We may be able to buy it outright in a few months." The next thing I heard was that "Blunden Harbour" had been purchased by the National Gallery.

"Emily," I scolded, "what about our option?"

She looked sheepish.

"Well," she answered, "I decided you should not pay so much for a picture and anyway, such big totems should be in a gallery and not in a home."

I believe she felt a little guilty nonetheless, as later on in the afternoon she gave me a small plywood forest sketch in unspoken compensation.

Now when I visit the National Gallery I look at "Blunden Harbour" with almost proprietary interest. On the whole, though, I am glad she did not let us have it, as it is one of the few of her canvases done entirely from a photograph—perhaps the only one. I knew this because one day when I dropped into her studio, she was sitting before the easel putting the last touches to this canvas. Tacked on the right side of the easel frame was a photograph of fair size. She had painted her own background but the totems themselves, the wharf and the canoes, were taken from the photograph, with only superficial change.

Frederick and I took up residence in Vancouver. From then on, Victoria was to be my home no more. I was there often for visits but the more intimate phase of my life with Emily was over. We corresponded constantly, however, (the bulk of my letters are from this period) and in Vancouver I found that I could be of practical assistance to her by helping out with showings of her work.

For there were two more interesting exhibitions in the University Library organized by Frederick and Hunter Lewis. The first of these, held in February 1936, included, in addition to Emily Carr's paintings, works by nine other Victoria and Vancouver artists: F. H. Varley, C. J. Scott, J. W. G. MacDonald, W. P. Weston, J. Delisle Parker, Max Maynard, Jack Shadbolt, Vera O. Weatherby and myself. Emily contributed field sketches and several canvases including "Blunden Harbour" which Dr. Sedgewick discussed fully in his opening remarks. He characterized the canvas as being exceptionally vigorous and well organized and pointed out how the sky, water and hills harmonized and balanced the forms of the totem figures.

The other exhibit took place in November 1938. It attracted wide attention. A photograph of "Cordova Drift" appeared in *The Ubyssey* along with articles by Frederick and a student. The student was obviously impressed, and wrote:

> This fusion of idea and subject, rendered as it is in terms of a penetrating analysis and by a vigorous originality of style, gives us the woods in essence—the rhythm of forest growth. These woods we have always known; Emily Carr makes us really see them.

This was a remarkably perceptive observation but it was not the only one of its kind. During these years there was much sympathetic and intelligent comment on her work. Liberal space was given her in the local press. The *Daily Colonist* and the *Daily Times* in Victoria and the Vancouver *Province* now recognized that she was news and reported newsworthy items about her, I thought, with a sense of pride in one of their unusual fellow-citizens.

Emily visited Frederick and me twice in Vancouver, on the occasions of her exhibits there, and it was a delight to entertain her. She was easy to please in social ways and very eager to meet the Vancouver artists. They, for their part, were just as anxious to see her again. C. H. Scott, J. W. G. MacDonald and W. P. Weston came to pay their respects and Nan Cheney dropped in often. Fred Varley, however, was her predilection for the moment and I used to drive her up to his studio high on a hill in North Vancouver for long talks and viewings of his paintings. People on the street smiled at the sight of Emily, a Queen Mary hat perched on her head, sitting sandwiched into the passenger seat of my cream cracker sports M.G.

Emily's second visit to us was to celebrate the first one-man showing of her work in Vancouver, in 1938. Reports about her successful exhibits at the University Library had filtered downtown to the Vancouver Art Gallery and were at least partly responsible for the decision to hold this one-man show. It was one of the highlights of her life. For the first time in British Columbia Emily had received unstinted praise and, after her return home, she wrote jubilantly, "I am simply *overwhelmed.* Isn't it beyond *extraordinary* selling seven.... I could never have believed that an exhibition of me could have met with such warm response."

Emily's reaction to publicity was not always so favourable. Frederick and I decided, at one point, that a little added coverage would do no harm. It was not easy to obtain her permission, as one of her major hates was attached to journalists. It is difficult to say whether or not her attitude was genuine. In any case, it was violent. The write-ups after the exhibitions at the University and Vancouver Gallery had mollified her somewhat but she was still antagonistic. She did, however, give her con-

sent for Hunter Lewis to write an account of her life and work
for the Vancouver *Province*. Professors were in her favour just
then, and she even co-operated. She sent over a photograph
and supplied material.

I then asked Ken Drury, Editor of the *Victoria Daily Times*,
to print a story and he sent Miss Ruggles to interview her. This
venture was less successful. Emily changed from a lamb to a
lion. Miss Ruggles quite innocently antagonized her and she
boiled over in a letter to me; it was full of underscoring. "I'm
sorry, Edythe, I was beastly awful. She was such a total *fool*. I
could have taken to bed with the pip .... She pranced all over the
house *unbidden* .... I hate those noisy, ignorant fools and frightful rubbish. Hate them like venom. If they would just stick to
work and not mix you into a filthy pudding of sentimentali-
ty. They try to show off their *own profound* knowledge which
is only a mess of art jargon that debases art." Nevertheless a
lengthy article did appear.

My ambition began to grow. I had read so much about
Gertrude Stein helping artists of promise that I decided to try
to interest her in Emily's work. She lent me three paper sketches and I packed them off to Paris. They were away for a good
year and were returned in a battered condition, unopened. A
letter from Alice B. Toklas informed me that Miss Stein was
too busy to give the matter any consideration. Emily wrote a
letter to comfort me in my disappointment. "I think she is a
blighter with a swollen head and rude into the bargain. But,
never mind. We've learned to leave Gerties alone and need not
think of her again. I think she might at least have spared an
eye-stare and jeer. My work seems fated, in a way, not to reach
the eye of the crits. First Roger [Fry] and then Gert. Well, what
does it matter as long as one can go on working? Perhaps it is

so that their smashing criticisms should not completely mince my heart."

In the meantime Emily was beginning to show signs of the approaching illness which eventually made her a semi-invalid. The tenants, the furnace, the stairs were beginning to tax her strength seriously and she made up her mind to dispose of the Simcoe Street house. At first she considered turning it into a People's Art Gallery, hoping the city would pay her a modest rental, but the scheme was a failure. In my opinion, all her hopes and plans for making art accessible to the "little people" were based on a misconception. The well-to-do, influential Victorians had always been at best apathetic towards her work but tradesmen calling at her door had sometimes asked to see her pictures and, as she felt this request was made from genuine interest in art, she conceived the idea that a gallery for the ordinary man was really needed. She discussed this plan with me, as with other friends, and I tried to persuade her to abandon it. I couldn't say so, but it seemed to me that the interest of the coal carrier, the garbage collector and the butcher, was more curiosity about Emily herself, her dogs and her studio than any hungering after pure art. Her way of life was so natural and necessary to her that she was quite unconscious of the fact that many "ordinary people" regarded her as something of an oddity. This plan, therefore, half idealistic and half practical, was doomed to be abortive from the very start.

In 1936, after twenty-two years of toil and trouble, she got rid of the House of All Sorts by exchanging it for a single, rentable, uncomplicated house in the Fairfield district. She received a twenty-five-dollar monthly income from this house and found for herself an old-fashioned, drab gray cottage on Beckley Street, in a rather poor district. She had many discouraging struggles with the Beckley Street house until she made it conform to her needs, but she grew to love it in the end. It had basic, marked advantages. The rent was only twelve dollars a month, the windows were high and gave good light for painting, and it was only a stone's throw from the old family home and from Alice's house. It was fine, too, for Woo and the pups and for the four new bantams which she had brought home from a sketching trip at Albert Head to eat up the earwigs. She loved to hear their crowing in the morning and their chortling in the yard.

At first, she was consumed with loneliness in her cottage. Remarks in her letters show how few friends she had and, consequently, how little interest was shown in her work even then, only nine years before her death. She wrote on March 8 of 1936: "I seem to be enveloped in a dull ache composed of tiredness, homesickness and loneliness .... I like the cottage though it does seem lonesome and drifting not to have tenants to do for. I don't feel as if I belonged to a soul or mattered on the earth." Later in the fall, she wrote from Albert Head: "I wish you were to be here for the winter, 'I ain't got nobody now.'"

Nevertheless Emily Carr and her work were gradually becoming known. Prominent people sought out her studio and sales came sometimes from unexpected sources. Mrs. Leopold Stokowski, wife of the celebrated conductor, visited the Beckley Street house to choose a canvas. My sister Ruth (Mrs. L. P. Herrington) of New Haven, Connecticut, bought one, and Lawren Harris purchased her famous "Indian Church" which was later sold to Mr. C. S. Band of Toronto. Mr. Band himself went to see Emily and selected three canvases to take East, for prospective buyers. One was "Lillooet Indian Village," (which was bought by Mr. Southam for $150). The second was a woods thing, "Goldstream Park." And the third was one of her favourites, "Swirl," which she hated to part with. Mr. Band later bought other canvases, among them "Nirvana" (two totems in a forest) for which he paid $200. Emily deeply appreciated his interest and assistance.

Numerous other smaller canvases were sold locally. At long last, her public and sales were increasing and she was getting much higher prices for her work. But her health was flagging, even though her will to work and produce was not. She was often despondent and sometimes almost collapsed under the weight of her weariness. She was advised to curtail her activities but could not, so the doctor, in desperation, ordered her to spend a whole day in bed each week just resting. She cheated a little, but on the whole obeyed his instructions and did improve.

During one of these rest periods, on a cool August day in 1937, Emily wrote me a long letter describing an exciting visit she had had from Lady Tweedsmuir. She had her "children," the two dogs Pout and Matilda, in bed with her as she wrote and her little blue lovebird Joseph was in his cage tucked in the corner behind her pillows.

Poor Emily had lived through an agonizing half hour before the important car arrived. The man opposite was in the habit of sitting outside half naked and she waited with alarm for his appearance. An "awful Chinaman's vegetable wagon with lean horse and flapping, torn curtains" decided just then to halt before her gate but "he moved on to make way for Royalty, thank the Lord." Lady Tweedsmuir, Emily wrote, had been accompanied by her lady-in-waiting and an equerry. They stayed for an hour and the equerry pulled out sketch after sketch from the racks and exhibited them on an easel. Lady Tweedsmuir was interested in a paper sketch and bought it. Emily had neglected to sign the sketch, however, so the equerry had to bring it back for correction of this omission and the chauffeur came again on that same evening to pick it up. (She told me later that the chauffeur had seen an old brass warming pan hanging just inside her front door on one of his first visits and when he came alone to pick up the sketch he bargained for it. She sold it to him for five dollars.) She pictured Beckley Street as being quite out of breath at seeing the Vice-regal car in front of her door three times in one week.

The year 1940 dawned with news as bleak as the weather. The landlady wanted to sell the Beckley Street house and Emily faced another upheaval. She was disconsolate. To me, to almost anyone else, this dreary cottage in its desolate and disorderly setting on the "wrong side of the tracks" in James Bay would have spelled disaster—something to flee from as quickly as possible. But Emily loved the ugly duckling. A little frumpy herself, she felt that she and the house had much in common. She mothered it, coaxed and patted it, then wriggled around inside until it fitted the idiosyncrasies of her way of life like the spiral shell of a snail.

Undisturbed by the demands and complaints of tenants, Emily had spent her four best, peaceful and productive years in this cottage. They had been years of steady and mounting acclaim and fame. She wept with regret as much as fatigue when she said good-bye to Beckley Street in February to move to Alice's house on St. Andrew's Street, in the "select" part of James Bay. She had come full circle. She had returned to live out her remaining invalid years a few steps from the large house in which she had been born—a house, incidentally, that is now being restored as an historical site.

Alice's house was her great pride and joy. She was extraordinarily possessive about it and pathetically worried that she would somehow lose her hold over it when Emily, with her stronger and more domineering personality, moved in. Although devoted to one another, the three Carr sisters had a deep-seated fear of losing their cherished independence. Since they had always maintained separate homes, this new arrangement of sharing a house was fraught with danger, even though Emily and Alice occupied separate quarters. Alice was easily hurt, Emily was easily ruffled, and there were many skirmishes before they settled down amicably.

As was her way, Emily created the atmosphere she needed for her work. Although the house was old and drafty, the little iron stove gave out a fine heat and made the bedroom and studio snug and cozy. Objects and animals found their right niche. The colourful lovebirds cooed in their aviary on the verandah. Miss Emily Carr was "at home" and at work again.

The clouds gathered around Emily quickly in those years. Between 1939 and her death in March 1945, she had two heart attacks and two strokes which brought great suffering. Although she was often despondent, sometimes flooded in tears, her courage rarely failed. She refused to give up. She painted as long as she could crawl to her easel and in 1942 went on a sketching trip to Mount Douglas against doctor's orders.

She was even deprived of the companionship of some of her creatures, as their care was too great a strain on her failing health. Her aviary was the first to go. Only two dogs were kept, and finally even Woo, the *enfant terrible*, was sent to Vancouver to live out her days in the company of strange monkeys in Stanley Park.

Emily begged me in her letters to visit Woo as she was sure that a familiar voice would comfort her and make her feel less captive. To please Emily, I went to the zoo several times and found Woo looking almost indecently naked without her habitual pinafore, but otherwise in fine fettle. She hurled herself from one limb of the monkey tree to another, chattering noisily all the time, and paid no attention to my entreaties at all. Not a glimmer of recognition after so much time spent together! Being fond of Woo despite the many pranks she had played on me, I found myself feeling hurt and a little indignant. In the end I had to admit that she was perhaps happier with her own kind than she had been in our company, but I carefully refrained from telling Emily so.

*f*aced with the fact that her painting was henceforth curtailed, Emily turned more and more to her second talent—writing. She had been dabbling in words most of her life but now that she was forced to spend many hours in bed she had the time to devote to concentrated work on her writing.

As a girl Emily had loved to confide her observations, her hopes and fears, her joys and sorrows to her diary. An emotional, inhibited child, she poured into her diary all her pent-up feelings. But her eldest sister, Edith, did not approve of secrets. One day she opened the book. She scolded and ridiculed Emily who was hurt, angry and humiliated to have her innermost thoughts bared to an unsympathetic eye. So she closed the cover on her girlish outpourings forever.

But the desire to express her thoughts did not die. It lay

dormant for most of her youth, only coming to the surface occasionally under the stress of emotion, when she would sit down and write a poem, a jingle, or a skit.

While she was in a sanatorium in England, recuperating from over-strenuous studies in London, she wrote, in doggerel verse, a humorous account of the sanatorium life. She illustrated the work with cartoons and it proved immensely popular with the staff and patients. Years later when *Pause: A Sketch Book* was published, pages of the sketch book appeared as illustrations.

Periodically throughout her life Emily produced similar little books based on her travels or her adventures. One such journal was written about a trip Emily and Alice made to Alaska and the Yukon when Emily was about thirty-five years old. They travelled from Seattle through the inside passage as far as Sitka on Baronoff Island and their freighter made frequent stops at small ports, canneries and unspoiled Indian villages. They stopped over in Skagway, an upstart town of tumbledown shanties and wobbly wharves, where just a few years before prospectors had left their ships to plod painfully over the old Klondyke trail in search of gold. The gold Emily found was of a different sort. In deciding on this journey, she had been influenced by the prospect of discovering the wealth of totems and Indian artifacts to be found in the villages on this wild stretch of coast. She felt that she must see for herself and actually "feel" these inscrutable totems in their natural setting if she were to fully grasp and interpret their grim reality. The scenic wonders of the inside passage also came as a revelation and she was staggered by the whole experience. The Alaska journal, very light and gay in mood, was the record of the sum of her impressions of this trip. Excerpts from it were published in the Victoria *Daily Colonist* in 1953. James Nesbitt wrote the story and the selections of entertaining verse were illustrated by comic watercolour cartoons, three to each article.

When she returned to Victoria from England early in 1905 Emily made her first foray into journalism. Engaged by the fledgling newspaper, *The Week*, she entertained its readers for almost a year with her witty cartoons and comments on current affairs.

During the long "blue period" of Emily's life, when the demanding tenants consumed all her energy and patience and she had to turn to her dogs, pottery and hooked rugs to keep herself afloat, she had no time to think of the deep, joyful things of life which were almost entirely submerged in her everyday frustrations. But the creative urge still nagged and could not be fully stilled by humdrum activities. At times she tried to put some of her long-bottled-up memories into words. They came pouring out without much regard to style, grammar or spelling. She read her stories to a few close friends, including myself, hoping hungrily for guidance and a little encouragement. We could all see that a real talent was struggling for expression but Emily herself was humble and deeply troubled by her technical faults. She felt that her workmanship was shoddy.

One evening, in 1926, after reading "Tombstones" to Flora Burns, Emily suggested that they should enroll together in a correspondence course in short story writing. Flora allowed herself to be persuaded and they both applied for membership in the Palmer Institute of Authorship in Los Angeles. The study material was not long in coming. Flora was working full time then and was too busy to finish the course, but Emily, with her usual drive, raced through it. Many of the stories published later on were written as exercises for this course.

Eight years later, still feeling the need of more formal training, she took another course in short story writing at the Victoria Summer School. She turned out to be the star pupil in the class! One of her stories "The Hully-up Letter" was warmly praised for its fine literary style and carried off the first prize. Pleased as punch, she was nevertheless horrified at the prospect of having to read her story at the closing exercises of summer school. She waited out the intervening days with anxiety, but when the time finally came to get up and read her Indian story to the would-be authors sitting in rows before her, she was so intent on making herself heard through the bad acoustics of the hall and in getting the central idea of the story over to her audience that she quite forgot to be nervous. The clapping, the bouquet of flowers and the enthusiastic appreciation was a heady accolade. It gave her the confidence she needed to carry on with her writing.

The pile of stories grew. But there were always fresh ideas and she was impatient to set them down on paper. When she was seated at her crotchety typewriter, searching for elusive letters and punctuation marks, her thoughts raced far ahead of her fingers and she decided to take a course in typing. She enrolled in the Sprott-Shaw business school in downtown Victoria and settled her plump form among the giggly girls who filled the room. Consternation and curiosity reigned! Emily pecked away conscientiously at the keys, resolved to master the touch system, but the "young things" easily outstripped her. She became discouraged and felt unhappy in the uncongenial company of sniggering students. Her patience wore thin and her fingers grew weary. She finally gave up, confronted her machine with resignation, and somehow managed to complete the manuscripts with her old self-taught method.

After she made the trip East in 1927 she began to keep journals—"jotting books" in which she tried to analyze and formulate her thoughts and impressions. Her journals were also a record of her experiences, many of them amusing, for Emily never failed to find herself in "situations" and she could almost always laugh at herself.

The whole tempo of Emily's life was speeded up after 1927. She wrote and painted like a woman possessed: the urge to create while there was still time drove her ruthlessly on. She sought new techniques to express her fresh vision. She struggled to strip her material down to its essence. Story followed story, one version after another.

Frederick very early became aware of her talent. He stole a little time from mathematics in class one day and read a couple of her stories to his students, to test their reaction. This was their first public reading. He prevailed upon Dr. Garnet Sedgewick to try the same experiment with his English students.

After the class readings, Emily timidly asked Dr. Sedgewick to give an opinion of her writing. She was afraid that he would find her illiterate and her subject matter dull and awaited his verdict with impatience and anxiety. After a great deal of prodding from Frederick and me and a flurry of distraught letters from Emily, it finally came. He was delighted with the stories but feared they would not find a *big* appreciative audience, although they deserved it. He agreed, however, to read several of her stories over the radio and the reaction of the air audience was good. Shortly after this, a CBC executive, Ira Dilworth, who had become a close friend of Emily's, wrote to his friend, W. H. Clarke, President of Clarke, Irwin & Company Limited and Manager of Oxford University Press, telling him about

Emily's work and his wish for him to see it. He did this partly because Emily had already submitted part of it to another publisher and had been terribly upset when a portion had disappeared for some months before it had been found. (It had been used as packing for a shipment of school books.) Mr. Clarke at once saw the charm of her writing, and although it was wartime and Emily was 69, felt it should be put in print at once. Emily was then hard at work on her autobiography which was to be called *Growing Pains* and on her journals which were to be published many years after her death under the title *Hundreds and Thousands*.

The first book of sketches, *Klee Wyck*, was published in 1941 and enjoyed immediate success with public and critics alike. A little later, to Emily's utter disbelief, it won the Governor-General's award for general literature. The University Women's Club honoured her and *Klee Wyck* by giving a large tea-party to celebrate her seventieth birthday. Other organizations sent messages of congratulation, and letters were read from prominent citizens, including the Lieutenant-Governor and the Mayor. It was a memorable and rewarding afternoon and Emily, wearing a bright corsage, was almost smothered in flowers and affection. She was touched by the continual flow of good wishes and, as she stood to thank the club, she was near tears and her voice was choked with emotion.

More acclaim followed. *The Book of Small* and *The House of All Sorts* appeared, and her autobiography was complete.

Emily was amazed at her sudden popularity. The same Victorians who had condemned her painting now praised her books. She kept up the pretence of hating publicity, of being disgusted and impatient with honeyed praise. But she had lost much of her toughness and was more mellow. Indeed, she sometimes looked as proud as a pouter pigeon as she listened to unaccustomed words of commendation. For the few short years she had left, though she was ill and very weary, Emily could bask in the sunshine of appreciation. Recognition had come to her at last, both as a writer and as a painter.

*I*t so happened that I was destined to share Emily's lean years but not her time of triumph. After the outbreak of the war, I was only in Victoria twice, once when my mother died in 1941 and again in 1944 when my father took ill and I stayed with him until his death. Up to that time we had corresponded but, after 1940, not with the previous regularity or even with the same warmth. I was far away and our interests had taken divergent paths. She was completely wrapped up in her writing, a part of her creative life that I had contacted only in the initial stages. Nevertheless, we had many a good visit together in 1944 and I brought what small comfort I could to a desperately sick old lady who clung courageously to a life which was full of pain. She was almost continuously in bed, often in tears, but she still had the spirit to call herself a "maudlin old fool" and would overcome her moods of despondency to write again and to paint a little. Her breath came in short, difficult gasps, her speech was affected and her left arm paralyzed, but she kept up the fight. Sometimes—an old story—she complained about her lack of friends: "Nobody wants to come to see an old, sick woman." Then she would gaze at a photograph

Emily Carr seated on her verandah with one of her dogs, circa 1944, photo by Edythe Hembroff

of Ira Dilworth on the wall of her bedroom and a soft look would come into her eyes, a look of unspoken gratitude, as if his help and friendship had made up for everything. On good days, she sat by the window and looked out into her little garden. With my help, she sometimes walked to the verandah where the aviary now stood empty and on one of those occasions I took a last picture of her with one of her dogs in her arms.

I knew when I left Victoria at the close of that year that I would never see her again. This unspoken thought lay heavy between us on the melancholy afternoon of parting. I put off leaving as long as I could, seeking for words which would express my gratitude and my affection but I was choked with emotion and no words came. Finally I put my arms around her and kissed her, then ran out of the door and down the steps with tears in my eyes.

a letter

FROM EDYTHE TO EMILY

Note: This letter was not included in original book.

102 Redpath St.
Ottawa, Ont
April 1, 1944

My dear Emily,

Your nice letter arrived today – I was only upset that it didn't contain better news although your old fighting spirit was still very much in evidence as were your pithy statements and emphatic underlinings. I hope your letter wasn't censored by the Jubilee hospital. It must be pretty bad. I guess all hospitals are these days. Even two years ago when I had my emergency op. in Winnipeg I had to threaten to throw something through the glass door before I got any service. Unfortunately the Jubilee doors have no glass in them if I remember correctly. And I don't suppose you have the energy for such gymnastics anyway. I am so sorry that you have not been strong enough to write. I hope when you next write to me you will be well enough to think out another story. You must have a lot of tales yet that want telling. And a little creative work is wonderful convalescent activity.

I can well imagine that it would be hopeless at home with Alice looking after things. I suppose the "old fool" has long since departed. Surely girls will be more plentiful soon. They seem to be here... and certainly food and materials are moving more freely – I've had no trouble lately getting tomato juice for instance – and there was none at all all winter. I send as much as I can to Frederick... as he will miss his fruits and vegetables very much.

I expect F is working very hard... but I haven't had a letter since he started his course...so I have no news to pass on. All I know is that he arrived safely and spent his first week-end in London with relatives. He has no doubt seen and heard a few bombs since he arrived. I hope I have another letter soon. I certainly find my apartment only half a home now. I haven't heard any news from the Coast for a long time. Does Nan still write to you? The Mrs Duncan here who takes Varley under her wing is a friend of hers. I heard that Ira was here again a couple weeks ago. I didn't see him of course. I wonder if he has a chance of being made the new president of C.B.C.?

Still no sign of spring here. It is snowing and today the first of April! On Monday we had 6 inches! The East is a poor place to live.

And now just more warm good wishes. I think of you very often – and hope you will not have another bad patch for a long time.

Affectionately,
Edythe

letters

FROM EMILY CARR

Note: the footnotes to these letters are the originals, added by Edythe Hembroff-Schleicher in 1969.

4 Oct., 1933
Victoria B.C.

Dear Edythe,

Your card received to-day. I did get one letter from you after you had been gone for a long time but no card till to-day. Am glad you are at your destination safe and sound and find the babe satisfactory. My word! A splendid trip like that and you have nothing to say about it. Your letter in fact sounded bored. You said you had nothing to write about. I give it up. You young folks don't know how to enjoy. You get too much. At your age and now too I could get more adventure thrills going from Victoria to Saanich and see something interesting and funny too.

I have had a high hop day. My friends the Cosiers are here from New York and have spent a long day with me—dinner and supper, three of them, and at supper time the boiler pipe burst as a pleasant little surprise. While I was sloshing around in six inches of water investigating, Woo got to devil's tricks upstairs and the whole establishment went into general bedlam. All dinners were arrested for lack of water while I swam around the basement performing on the taps and I nearly kissed the plumber when he discovered it was only a pipe, not the boiler. They cost so much.

I have been very busy getting off my exhibition for Edmonton—25 paper sketches for a civic exhibition and the 12 canvases for the University exhibition. The sketches I backed with mosquito-netting bound with white paper and put half-round stick top and bottom like maps and they looked fine and are strong. Mrs. McVicker[1] came to stay for three nights and I mounted sketches to the tune of her croak. She was very bright and happy though, and I quite enjoyed her. And she was tickled at being away three whole days. Her teeth are out and her breath sweeter. Now I must finish three canvases for the Group in Nov. They will need shipping in two weeks.

Lee Nam[2] has been having a show in China Town. I call it very sporting of him and thought his exhibit charming. I went four times and took people. He is a nice little chap. I invited him over to see the Edmonton sketches and he gave me some fine crits. He *knew* what he felt and why. He squatted China-wise on the floor and went over each sketch. There were 46. I found him helpful. The same day afterwards Max and Evelyn[3] came and made me weary. I told Max to pick out all things he saw blatantly wrong. Well of all the....! His crit wasn't worth a sniff. He picked on one wretched little hut and havered over its not being quite in place for half an hour, Evelyn catching this silly jargon and pol-parroting every syllable. People who don't paint cannot criticize. How can they! They string words that they have heard, phrases and art jargon, but there is no meat in it, only fuzz like "cow-brand" in lemonade—nip but no substance.

The weather is now heavenly—Indian summer. September was wretchedly wet and cold. I must go out and see how the "Elephant" is getting on. I am wintering her in the country near Four Mile House. The lot next to me is too difficult to get her out of. She is very comfortable and lovely to live in but she

---

1   *Mrs. McVicker,* an old friend of Emily's who previously owned an antique shop in Victoria. (Mentioned more fully in the text.)

2   *Lee Nam,* a young artist whom Emily sponsored and mothered for a time.

3   *Max and Evelyn Max Maynard,* a young Victoria artist, and his former wife. Max is now a Professor of English at the University of New Hampshire in the United States.

is not very easy to move about. The Flats are nice for warm weather but very damp and too many Sunday picnics there.

Henry[4] made the first part impossible to work and then the weather broke. I did sketch but nothing startling. The Flats strike me as incongruous. The immense trees are of a different time and place to the other stuff. There is no second growth to fill the gap. It is being very spoiled by gravel and wood breaks. In and out all the time mutilating and destroying roads, peace and growth.

I have not seen your mother since you left. Good luck.

M. Emily Carr

P.S. Arts and Crafts have a show this month. I shan't show unless there is a modern room and they need help to fill up. They had quite a representative show at the Willows. Mr. Chickley ran it and Arts and Crafts had nothing to do with it. I was away and did not go—lent 6 canvases. From the newspaper it seemed very representative of local *masters* and *mistresses*. Mrs. Parker lent a group of Delisle's[5] things. My sisters came home much wrought up by the things of Max. I asked him what they were but he said only old ones. He has done little this summer (except talk). He threatens to invite me up to see but never does. Jiggers—the artists about *are slack*.

---

4   *Henry,* Henry Brand, my former brother-in-law. (Mentioned more fully in the text.)
5   *Delisle,* Delisle Parker, well-known local artist, one of the few who were sympathetic to Emily's work.

My dear Edythe,

Well here I am returning from a visit of nine days to Toronto.
I go back to Chicago and straight out to Victoria. Reach Chicago
at 8:30 p.m., leave 10:30.

What do you suppose joyful thing I am taking home? No
less than one of Lawren Harris's[6] Arctic sketches! I am thrilled
from boots to hat. He gave me my choice of several but we both
(he and I) picked this. I do feel so proud and happy to possess
it. His Arctic pictures are simply glorious. I spent three long
afternoons in his studio, and he showed me everything he had.
And best yet, I had dinner at his home. It's simply wonderful
and beautiful arrangements: stripe lighting—and crowning all,
his pictures in the beautiful quiet setting.

I suppose you do not know I was met in Chicago by Mr.
Stickley's friend who informed me on the platform the exhibition of pictures was closed on my nose—twelve hours before.
Well, it was a blow and I felt like returning right smack—but
decided I should see what was to be seen though it was all
nothing really to me. I just went for the pictures. They only
advertised the closing of the gallery two days before. Lawren
Harris wired me the moment he knew but I had already left.
But I do not mind now as I would not have been able to go to
Toronto otherwise, and I had such a grand time there, and they
were all so good to me.

---

6   *Lawren Harris,* Group of Seven artist who for a time greatly influenced and helped
Emily.

I stayed a week in Chicago. Saw all the sights and the Fair three times. It did not impress me much though there were some wonderful things to see. The herbage was all dead—trees, shrubs, flowers—the paint splashed off the buildings. The weather *bitter* cold. Rain and wind. Still I extracted some fun from it but six days sent me violently home-sick. So I got the notion I'd trot off to Toronto. I did not even finish out the week I had paid for. I wired Mrs. Housser[7] and went. And what a wonderful welcome I got. I stayed with the Houssers. It is a wonderful home. All books and pictures and lovely talks and people. Bess gave a big tea. Almost everyone artists—about 40 or 45. I knew most of them. Many delightful lunches, teas, dinners followed but Bess was dear and did not accept more than we could do without over-weariness, and I had two or three evenings at home with them for long good talks or reading aloud. We went to hear Kreisler one night after a lovely little dinner at Miss McLaughlin's[8] very modern and charming flat. She is lovely. She had bought one of my pictures two years ago and is a great friend of Bess's.

The Group of 28 Show was interesting. It did not come up to the Group of Seven Shows by a long way. Lacked their dignity and unity—but there was interesting stuff there all the same. I wonder if you will get down to see it and if you know when you return out West yet. I shall have to get busy when I get back. What a lot of time I have spent away from home this year! I am returning very keen to renew the struggle in spite of the fact my things looked awful there. I saw Jack Shadbolt[9] and

---

7   *Mrs. Housser,* Bess (Mrs. Fred Housser), later second wife of Lawren Harris.
8   *Miss McLaughlin,* Isabel McLaughlin, well-known Toronto artist and collector.
9   *Jack Shadbolt,* now a famous Vancouver artist and teacher.

John MacDonald[10] yesterday. Jack has a small job teaching two nights a week in some school and seemed in fair spirits and as know-it-all as ever.

I seem to have been away aeons of time but in reality will be home three weeks to the day I left. It has been cold weather with snow. Day coach travelling is very wearisome. I will now try to snooze.

You asked what I thought of the architecture. Well, it was interesting, but by the time I got there it was shabby and dilapidated.

Now I am off to the dining-car.

Hope to hear from you soon,
Yours, Mom

---

10 *John MacDonald,* long-time admirer of Emily Carr, a student of aesthetics. Now Professor of Spanish, University of British Columbia.

Dear Edythe:

Three cheers for Dr. Sedgewick[11] and three more when the tin comes through. I can't for the life of me remember which Lillooet one I sent over but, anyhow, I am tickled pink. Sales are sufficiently infrequent to be thrills these lean days, No, don't bother to post sketches if Helen[12] will kindly bring them back when she comes. Also no hurry about book.

You are very sporty giving a lecture. I admire your pick-up-and-get—always up to some ruction and making most of your talents. Your house sounds very attractive. You never mention the Lewises.[13] Do you see much of them now?

Still sitting in my field. There were five days of *complete pour* but I sat on. Used to tuck myself up on the bed, put tins round to catch the drip and work, read, write and watch the rain come down. It's assorted now—dew, shine, blow, cloud. I'm working but have not been feeling very good. Troubles below the waistline, due to ructions in the liver, I suppose, and beastly back aches that kick at walking. I did get as far as my woods today. Other days I have been working in the dip beside the van. The sea and sky have been naughty; sulky and drab with fogs. I have been changing my size because only two shapes in an exhibition of sketches gets very monotonous. I did a *bad* square this morning and a small wretch this morning. Both rubbish

---

11 *Dr. Sedgewick,* Dr. G. G. Sedgewick, then Head of the English Department, University of British Columbia. (Mentioned in text.)
12 *Helen,* Helen Hembroff Ruch, my sister.
13 *The Lewises,* Hunter and Stella Lewis. Hunter, a Professor of English at the University of British Columbia, was helpful in introducing Emily's work to the University and Vancouver. (Mentioned in text.)

but as I did real study on them I don't care. Monday, being first day since the deluge and too wet to sit out, I went into town and saw my family.

I seem to have been lazy out here this time, other than painting. Most days I go to the McMinns'[14] some time or other and this takes up time. Sometimes I go out at night but always grudgingly as it is much cosier in the van. So dark and dreary coming into a big field full of dark and footholes and then a cold, black van. Mrs. McM. is finding Albert Head a snarling, unfriendly community. They *are* "catty." I fancy next year I shall try Saanich Peninsula. There is a caravan advertised in tonight's paper. Buy it and come along! What fun!

I got paint in town Monday. Will borrow a ladder and paint the van top before shutting up for the winter. Mr. Wilkes says I can leave her here. It is as good as anywhere. I wish you were to be in Victoria for the winter. "I ain't got nobody now," but am taking home three bantams to eat earwigs. Now it's the disreputable hour of 9:45. I got up between six and seven, lit "little smelly" and made a cup of tea, then had tea and melba toast breakfast in bed as it is so sousing and cold with dew in the early morning. In the evening, after sketching, I usually lie and read or write for a couple of hours but it is usually dark soon after six.

Well, here's good-bye and thanks for selling the sketch.

> *Affectionately yours and Fred's,*
> *M. Emily Carr.*

PS: Sure, use sketches or any part of me that's any use in your talk.

---

14 *McMinns,* owners of property where Emily parked her van.

316 Beckley St., Victoria,
March 8 (1936)

My dear Edythe:

I got out and in and am fairly settled. The last ten days were *awful*. Cleaning the old and the new. The workmen were impossible. If it had not been for Willie N.[15] I'd have curled up and died like a dead leaf when rain has washed out all its crisp.

The house has "points" (good and bad). It's too big for *me* and not big enough for my *possessions*. I never seem to be *in* the rooms but always going from one to the other. As for the cook stove!!???? burrrr! I think any soul who conquers a wood and coal range is a genius pure and simple. Mine sulks and burns *me* but not the wood which is wet and troublesome and I left a whole heap of splendid dry stuff in my basement. (I have to start boiling the breakfast kettle the night before.) The water also gives me great concern. There is *no* pressure. It trickles, and only *one* drop trickles at *one* time. I have seen people *cry* tears harder than that. They say the pipes are corroded and nothing can be done without new entirely. Oh well! It is happy that I am not a "family." The cottage is very bright with big, high windows and, of course, the rent is only $12.00 per month so you can't expect the up-to-dateist for that and it is fine for Woo and the pups. The studio is the size of an aspirin box. I am keeping it bare as possible so I can get in myself. It has never learned the ways of paint. Still, on the whole, I like the cottage, though it does seem lonesome and drifting not to have any tenants to do for. I don't feel as if I belonged to a soul or mattered on the earth.

---

15 *Willie N.*, Willie Newcomb, a loyal friend of Emily's, an expert in Indian lore. (Mentioned in text.)

I hear the proposed art exhibit at the University [of B.C.] is postponed indefinitely. I saw E. Brand[16] this a.m. She says you will be having Helen now, so I expect you are busy.

I had a long letter from Yvonne Housser[17] (at last). She had been to see my show at the Heliconian Club and really wrote a very nice and enthusiastic letter about the pictures. Said they were well received. Lismer[18] gave a lecture there while they were on the wall. On Modern Art. She said a Professor Helford, an Englishman who has the Chair of Fine Arts at the University and a very sensitive and intelligent person about pictures, asked the President how she enjoyed the lecture. She said, "To tell you the truth, I am so excited about these pictures, I could hardly pay any attention to anything else." He replied, "I feel exactly the same way." Also the instructor in Art at Upper Canada College was very interested. Fred and Yvonne themselves were "thrilled" they said and also that I would have been pleased had I heard the comments, so I guess it went off O.K. I felt that I got a much fairer idea than from Lismer who seemed sort of peeved. After the enthusiasm he exhibited when out West, I never feel him to be very stable. He undertakes too much and becomes unreliable.

It is cold and blistery. I took the dogs to the beach but it was too angry to stay. Things do not look nice in the papers today, do they? I suppose there will never be peace till there is a vast blow up. Sickening to contemplate.

My fire has gone out so I'll limp into bed. I never knew furnaces, even if run only part time, could change the atmosphere of a house so.

---

16   *E. Brand,* Edith Brand, my former sister-in-law.
17   *Yvonne Housser,* Yvonne McKague Housser, well-known artist, second wife of Fred Housser, writer on Canadian painting.
18   *Lismer,* Arthur Lismer, Canadian painter, member of the Group of Seven.

Are you coming back with Helen? You said you might be over sooner than you expected. It would be nice to see you. I wonder if anyone will ever come over here to see me now my studio is small and mean?

Woo keeps me busy reinforcing her cage and thinking up new door catches that she cannot master. I lost her the other day and found her in the oven! (Shows how grand it heats.) She shakes her coop till you'd think we were being bombarded.

Ever affectionately,
M. E. Carr.

PS: Write soon, I need cheer.

Monday—PS: How nice to get your letter this morning. Thank you for the housewarming note. Lovely of you to think of it. I think I shall be comfortable and happy here but, just at present, I seem to be enveloped in a dull ache, composed probably of tiredness, homesickness and loneliness. I laughed at you not wanting to stay alone during Fred's absence, with the voluble Mrs. B. below. You'd have a *fit* at six rooms of emptiness and a garden and a yard. But it is not "spooky" at all. I roam round inside and out all hours of light and dark. The bantams are content. They tried the next yard but came chortling home to me and now stay here. We have great conversations. The dogs like it here. So does Woo. So I must fall in line with the family. And, I do like the little house too, all except the water tap and the stove and quite so much lonesomeness.

So long for now,
M. E. C.

My dear Edythe:

Do I owe you or do you owe me? I don't know anyhow. I feel too rotten to do most anything so will inflict you with a miserable rigmarole. Beginning of last week I came down with flu; had a sniffy cold week before and seemed to get over it. Hudsons[19] all had flu so I suppose I got it there, though nearly everyone in the locality seems to have had, are having, or will have. It seemed to specialize in throats.

How went the Exhibition? Tell me about it. Six of my Indian pictures are going over to Vancouver for the Folk Show at the Van Hotel. The old man who has borrowed them for his Indian exhibit is three-quarters crazy and the other quarter looney and does not know any more about pictures than a fat hen. "Blunden Harbour" is among them.

I have done a little work. Stacked sketches opposite my bed and studied them when I was getting better. They're perfectly punk, seems like. Ruth Humphrey[20] was coming over this afternoon (she was coming last week, but I was ill), but this morning she phoned to say she is ill—cold. I was glad she did not come. I did not want to put her off again and talking is so painful. I have "D'Sonoqua" and two other stories ready for her to pull to pieces. I don't think it is a bit of use ever trying to do anything. With good writing I could never compete, and with the popular stuff, I have no interest. All the same, I do get great

---

19 *Hudsons,* Emily's next-door neighbours on Beckley Street.
20 *Ruth Humphrey,* former teacher at Victoria College and later Assistant Professor of English at the University of British Columbia.

enjoyment from writing. Things tease me inside till I tackle them. When they are once off my chest, I never think of them again. They quit tormenting. I am afraid I am dreadfully un-ambitious. Work does not seem to mean that to me; it's more of an easement. Selfish, I am afraid. It seems like a thing that should grow along *with* you. What you *do* does not seem to me to matter much, nor what you leave behind. But, anything that *sprouts* from your working—that matters. Most of us are dead as knobs nine-tenths of the time. Then, piff!! a little something bursts and the juice runs out.

That is all that is worth keeping and there is scarcely enough to dirty a bottle. A long letter from Lawren this week. They are still in New England and he still is doing abstracts. Bess is working too, but she has not written for a long time. I went to see Henry one day but he was out. I thought the Strathope Home looked very nice. The nurse said that Henry was as usual and pretty well. I have not seen Edith for a long time. I do not ask her to come because I know that what little time she has and I expect she is out all she can be with her young man.

Flora Burns[21] is in St. Joseph's. Had an operation, but she is doing splendidly. They said I could go and see her today, but I shall not till I am quite O.K. and, by then, she will be home.

Now there is no more to write about and I must write to Flora's sister in Montreal. That's my job.

Write soon. Come to think, it is your turn—*two times*—now.

One of my summer pupils wrote from Vancouver. Said she had been talking with Mr. Hood[22] who would like to have some

---

21 *Flora Burns,* an old friend of Emily's who helped her with her writing.
22 *Mr. Hood,* former Vancouver art dealer.

of my stuff for selling. Do you know him?

> *Love to you both,*
> *M. Emily Carr.*

> *316 Beckley St.*
> *Thursday, (November, 1936)*

Dear Edythe:

Thank you for prompt reply. Always my luck to be too late for Ex. You see I did not realize it was the Canadian Group showing. I thought it was just one of their National Gallery travelling exhibits wherein they usually display all Canada's third rate pictures. So I never thought of coming, but your entertaining description very much interested me. Well, it is better for my pocket not to go. I would not cross just to see Jack's, though I have no doubt it will be quite interesting and it's sporting of him to do it. I would like to have seen you both but it would have to have been a very rush visit, and as Mrs. Hudson is ill, it is lucky I am not going. I would not leave the pups twice per day for Alice. So, thank you just the same.

I am hilarious ! They have built me a new kitchen chimney so I won't have to move. It was done today. It has been bad the last two weeks. The kitchen so cold. So, when I paid my rent I gave notice to be withdrawn unless the owner fixed the chimney right away. I have just lighted the kitchen fire and it actually *crackled* so I hope when I have had the sweep and cleaned the pipes, I shall have comfort and be able to cook and hot-tub and wash.

Yesterday, May Macrae and Edith Parker called on me. They were both quite charmed with my lair. I think they expected to find me living in a barrel or something. I was all prepared for Ruth Humphrey and had a cosy fire in the front room. My flowers and ferns are so nice in there and it is nice to have a room to show visitors in without *passing* the studio. I always felt in Simcoe that it was a bit of a slap when I hurried impossible studio people past the door to the sitting room. I am enjoying Miss Humphrey so much and she says she's enjoying it too. She has given me such good help and ideas. I have written several short stories, little things that I feel are better and she finds no fault with them. She likes "D'Sonoqua's Cats" very much too and made a few small suggestions. "The Cow Yard" she condensed a lot, leaving out heaps. It spoils "The Cow Yard" for me but helped me a great deal in seeing how to tackle other things. She is not a bit hard and fast to rule and doesn't care a hang about *plots* but, after her three visits so far, I feel all keyed up to try again with keen enjoyment and from a slightly different angle.

I had not heard one word about the exhibition so your letter was very welcome. I do understand what you say about the Eastern group being posterish and a bit bizarre. The new group have tried to follow the old group. The old group were to start with commercial artists who burst forth and followed a real idea with an ideal ahead and they accomplished something—and something big. The new group were *admirers* of the old group and wanted to copy them but they had not the ideal within themselves. Their objective is different and not down in their roots. They paint to the old group's formula, whereas the old group utilized their commercial designing. The new group sort of took that as their finish. Oh, I don't know. All men are sheep, all sheep are fools and this includes women. Whether it was the praise and glory that turned the heads of the group, I don't know, but it seems to me they have all fallen down or stopped. They have lost something but perhaps this is just natural. They did their job and are now past. We all have to face that. We can't go on forever and must sit back and fold up and leave it to others to do the going on.

Willie came last night. I made him sit in the kitchen so we could *gloat* over the pop and crackle of the stove. Oh! goodness! goodness! It is *grand* to have a warm kitchen and hot water and an oven that would cook if it was asked. I'm so happy and it's a wet dismal day outside. I painted till dusk and then stretched eight canvases (utilized old picture frames, not very large ones) in the kitchen. First I had done in this house. I am working on a largish canvas. Summer sketches are all mounted. Mr. Kyle had two nice light cases made for me to ship paper sketches in. Hold twenty-five each. Should you want a set for showing at the University, you can have them. I am trying to get enough spunk to have an evening, but there are few to ask and I don't know how it would work out in the cottage. Ruth Humphrey wants me to. Well, I'll see. I would not hesitate if you folks were here.

I would like to have seen A. Y. Jackson's[23] stuff. I was a fool not to have known it was the same show as the one this year in the East. Did my papers not look tuppency among all the canvases? It was A. Y. Jackson who framed them I believe. You said awfully nice things but I'd like to have seen for myself how papery they looked beside the canvases. Too bad they sent poor ones of Lawren. I don't think he is exhibiting his abstracts yet. Bess wrote me a nice letter a few days ago. Also Lawren. They

---

23   *A. Y. Jackson,* Canadian painter, member of the Group of Seven.

are both working enthusiastically and each praises the other's work. I guess they have been pretty badly chewed in Toronto. Yes, Lawren Harris's son and daughter both paint. He thinks the daughter very clever—more daring. I liked young Lawren's work better. He is a nice chap. Quite young and now married— also the girl. Yvonne McKague is Mrs. Housser No. 2. She is counted very clever and is, I believe, an excellent teacher in the Art School. Bess thought a lot of her and her work but the stuff I saw in her studio did not specially interest me. Casson[24] and Carmichael[25] had a whole room of watercolours in one of the Group Shows. They were beautiful in colour and pattern. They were all twin brothers to all the rest of them and there they stopped, and you left the room feeling you had overeaten. I met both men at Lawren Harris's. They were small peevish-looking individuals, struggling to support families I guess.

Well, I must trot up to see Alice. Are you not coming down to Victoria soon? Christmas will be here before we know it.

Can you understand the folks who have to *kill* time? Life is like a whole packet of firecrackers going off at once without even waiting for the match.

You ought to see Matilda. She's the cutest yet. Quite different from Liza. Matilda is demure and very independent but affectionate. She's a smoothie.

Love to Fred and yourself
Be good, affectionately yours,
M. E. Carr

---

24   *Casson,* A. J., Casson, Canadian landscape painter, also a member of the Group of Seven.
25   *Carmichael,* Franklin Carmichael, another Canadian artist and member of the Group of Seven.

Dear Edythe:

Why don't you write? I phoned Mr. Hembroff tonight to ask if you'd gone South. I thought from your last letter you might have gone to Helen but he said Mrs. Hembroff was South so I presume you are not. No more will ink (or pencil) deface paper to you if you don't answer. You owe me two. This will be three. You don't have to wait for news. Anything about your work and life interests me.

I am awaiting an escort. It is pelting. I am being fetched to Margaret Clay's[26] to supper and after to a show at Miss Cann's[27] of Magic lantern pictures. I'd rather have a crust in the kitchen and a book, but these things must be I suppose. It's kind of Miss Cann.

I have been busy this week. A Mr. Band[28] (don't think I told you this before, if so, 'scuse) asked me to send him some pictures to see if one would fit his house. He pays all expenses and cartage and crating but Willie and I did that. The representative's man did not see any difference in packing oysters and canvases. They went Friday and Saturday comes a letter from Lawren with a cheque in it for a canvas. It seems a man always wanted the Indian Church but was too late. Lawren got it first. Now it is stored in the Toronto Gallery. The man is a Director and he saw it there among Lawren's pictures and asked him to

---

26   *Margaret Clay,* an old friend of the Carr family, Head Librarian of the Victoria Public Library.
27   *Miss Cann,* Jeanette Cann, former teacher of English at Victoria College and long-standing admirer of Emily's work.
28   *Mr. Band,* C. S. Band, former Director of the Toronto Art Gallery and well-known collector.

sell it to him. Lawren said it ought to be in sight, not hidden in the Gallery basement and the Harrises are not taking any pictures to the U.S. with them so, he said "yes" on one condition: that the man would will it to the Gallery when he died. He had intended to do that himself. Well, he sent the cheque right on to me and wants another canvas for his son in Toronto and gave me the horrible job of making choice for him. However, as those three are over there, there may be a solution of two to choose from if Mr. Band takes the other one. He may not like any. Never any knowing.

When are you coming over? The term must be almost over.

Yesterday has turned into today. I went. Margaret's supper was delicious and a delight. Dr. Lamb[29] and Ruth and Jack's girl, besides the family and me. Then on to Miss Cann's through a pelt of rain. Miss Cann was all spark. I suppose there were between 15–20. She, or rather Dr. Lamb, "majicked" in a big empty room below. Some of the pictures were very nice—some tripe. I was much disappointed in Miss Cann as a speaker. She had no sureness of her subject, rambled and apologized for everything, artists, pictures, intelligence and herself. She kept it up for two hours and what she had to say could have been said neatly in one-half an hour. Poor dear! I had great sympathy for her but I thought, being an English teacher, and I suppose a lecturer more or less, she'd have been more at home. She kept embarrassing me by asking my opinion. Asked me to spout and I told her I did not know much about pictures or artists. I mean it too. I *don't*. The History of Art and the things that are written about the men have never interested me greatly, I believe. Only the work. I think that each man's art is just his

---

29   *Dr. Lamb,* Dr. Kaye Lamb, British Columbia Provincial Librarian and Archivist, 1934–40. Later Dominion Archivist and National Librarian.

growth. Studying with a master, an artist may acquire some of his tricks and his technique. And his thoughts may be directed into the same channel. But, he cannot think his thinks because he's he and the other is the other. These critics give for fact what they can only surmise. How can they "feel" through the growing soul of the victim. He probably did not realize what was going on, himself. It's all talk instead of study these days. It seems to me that Miss Cann takes life hard anyhow. Flapping and gasping like a fish in a dry puddle. Well, I had better quit and make up the sleep I lost over the party and the coffee. The days are so short and dark. I miss the great light of the old studio though this little fellow might be a lot worse.

What think you of our King? We certainly don't want a female with three live husbands sitting on our throne. I'm sorry for him and can't believe he'd let his nation down.

Remember, this is the last epistle to the Brands till I hear, and all three are answered, even if I bottle up till I burst with news. For writing is a great escape valve with me.

Love and affection in the meantime,
M. Emily

St. Joseph's Hospital
Wednesday evening.
(February, 1937)

My dear Edythe:

You came in tulips at noon and in your dear, kind letter this afternoon. Both were lovely and so "youish." Fancy your asking me to go over to be loved and pampered by you. It was just splendid of you and Fred to have such a kind thought and I do appreciate it. But hospital is the place for me per present. Dr. McPherson told A. he should keep me here and not be in a hurry to send me home. Then, I am to have a woman and play "lady." For present, it is utter laziness with a good bit of dopey stuff as well as hypos when there is pain but attacks are getting less frequent. He told Alice I was a very sick woman but that he had known cases as bad to entirely recover. So, you see, maybe after a long rest, I will lead a fast life again. He is very attentive and kind. Everyone is good to me. It seems to be exertion and bodily effort my heart kicks at, making breath short and pain long. Oh! my flowers are lovely! I have had lots—all the luscious, hopeful ones and they are all just like their senders. Yours are the dead image of you. Cool, mauve, with warm beautiful hearts, with all sorts of sweet loveliness inside and mystery, and perfume. They are in a mauve basket full of the tenderest, smooth green and close by the bed. I can feel your love and Fred's oozing out of each bloom. Before I opened the box, I said "TULIPS." They smelled so rich. I have daffodils too, and chrysanthemums. I am lucky. Alice comes every afternoon and I see a few people but they don't let them stay long. My room is North and into a quiet court. Opposite are rooms full of the new-born, but though they yell hard sometimes, it's such a crazy, meaningless yap that it does not worry. Flat lozenges of "waaa" pouring out. I suppose the creatures must do something having come alive but, there's no pain and no common sense attached to their noises. The old Priest who groans on the opposite end of life next door is more trying but they say he does not hurt either. He is just groaning "out," as the others are waaing "in."

Love to both. Don't worry about me. I am lots better and

taking things day by day as they come. I can't realize there is a cold snap going on. My window is wide open and only one blanket. This complaint likes air.

Thanking you for everything you blessed dears. About cash—but I really have plenty; thank you all the same.

Yours,
M. E.

St. Joseph's, Sunday night
(February, 1937)

Dear Edythe:

What splendid friends I have! Thank you all for your work and interest in my behalf. It all worked out. Ruth met Mr. Newton[30] and took him to my house where Willie was in readiness with fires and pictures and Alice. After seeing little, (he said it would take him until midnight), he and Ruth came to hospital. Willie and I had been going over some letters etc., from the East, in the afternoon and I went pop suddenly and scared poor Willie. My own nurse came and then the head, whom I have dubbed Mrs. Snippet. I was dreadfully scared Mrs. Snippet was going to put a heavy foot on my evening visitors. I got round my own nurse and then Dr. McPherson came in. He was lovely and told me to go straight ahead, so Snippet got no look in. I was in a welter of exhaustion next

---

30   *Mr. Newton,* Eric Newton, English art critic for the *Manchester Guardian,* lecturer and author of many books on art. Among other posts he held that of Professor of Fine Arts at Oxford University and the Slade School of Art.

day but am much better today even though Willie brought five pictures up here to be signed, and a pot of paint and a brush like a whitewash brush, but we accomplished it. They are to go off at once. I don't understand matters yet. I can't believe the Gallery wants to buy them. I think it is just one of their borrowing spasms. I believe he was very enthusiastic (Mr. Newton). He and Willie worked till midnight and he said he wished he had another day to stay over. He only saw a very few of the sketches. Have not seen Ruth since. They all seemed to be scared to come. I'd love to have had a good talk with Mr. Newton. They said I could only see him a few minutes but, I thought him very sympathetic and understanding about work. I am surprised at some of his selecting. He wanted three big ones badly but they were three inches over the stipulated 50 inches so had to be cut out. Thank Frederick for his nice letter. I loved it. And Dr. Sedgewick for his kindness and Mr. Lewis too. What did Mr. Newton talk about? Did he see your work? And Max's and Jack's?

I'd better not write more. Head's gone mouldy. But, don't be disappointed if it's only one of Brown's[31] whims. You know I've experienced them before and shan't be disappointed if the poor old things are only just off on one of their vapid little toots.

Love, M. C.

PS: Woo and Tantie live in your city now.

Why don't you and Fred call me other than "Miss." Any of my epithets you fancy.

Home in bed.

---

31   *Brown,* Eric Brown, Director of the National Gallery in Ottawa.

Dear Edythe and Fred:

Congratulations from you to me! You don't know how delicious the cottage seems and *it is* good too. Willie has turned the front bedroom into the picture room with racks and also cut a door through to the studio. Now canvases are all so easy of access, and can be shown right there and put in racks with no trouble. Besides the little rack room makes a cosy little bedroom for the woman and saves having to have a fire in her room. So, that is economy. She's a nice person. Alice got hold of a practical nurse. I'm constantly being "pulsed," wrist, throat, temple, ear or knee. She takes much more care of me in a way than the hospital which was overcrowded and became bad. After being in bed six weeks all but two days, altogether in hospital five weeks, they rigged me up like an Aunt Sally, threw my clothes on and expected me to gallop away. No herding off in a wheelchair or exercise in the corridor. They only allowed me five minutes to get dressed in before the Hudsons were to come for me. So, I was all out of breath and exhausted after they had pounded into me the necessity of no hurry, worry or exertion. I just don't know how I got home, but I did. Mr. and Mrs. Hudson each side and Elinor behind. We mounted the steps and thank the Lord they were not the *old ones*. The moment I lit on the mattress of my own bed in my own house, I began to improve and lick my dishes clean. Mrs. Hassack is Scotch and kind and good to the dogs and very to me. Alice looks as if she's just dropped the cook stove after carrying it round in her arms for six weeks. Done nothing all day but lie and rest and just have one peek in the studio. To see the good, rich, old mud instead of the grey brick wall and the Hudsons' plum tree, even without a leaf, and their hideous garage, from my bed are a treat. I'm sure I'll get better on the run. Apparently I have to remember, though I'm hatched from the grub, it was with a pin through the body. Anyhow, if I can't fly, it's nice to flap.

Love to you both. I got your letter yesterday. How your weather does keep up. Too bad!

Yours, M. E.

Wednesday. Very tired this a.m. I believe it's now Lent which means Easter will be here which means you'll probably be down, which means it will be fine to see you. It's delicious having the little girl pups home. They tuck one each side of me in bed all day. Suppose I'm paying back for the exertion of getting home. Sister (hospital) thought I should have ambulanced but that costs $5.00 and I think the Hudsons' car was as good. They've been so kind. She's been often to hospital. You never have same nurse three times running. Some are good, some just pick-ups. No proper ones to be got. They're having a hard time and so are the patients, but there were already several empty beds.

Dear Edythe:

I seem to have slumped in letter writing lately. Not that I've "forgotted" you nor "press of business." But the days go—and I am so slow over the little I do. Slow dressing at 10:30, then a *rest, then a little* puttering around. *More rest,* lunch, *more rest,* a little typing (one-half hour) *then more rest.* At two p.m., retire to bed (unclothed, I mean ungeared). *Rest for one hour complete.* Visitors. *More rest.* Supper. More rest. Sometimes, if not too tired, dressing gown and a walk round rooms or a sit in the dark in the studio for an hour to cool off. Bed at nine. Some busy life, eh? But, I have been busy today interviewing new help. My good woman said she understood she was only engaged for a month after I came out of hospital and had other plans. I asked her to stay on over Easter as I want Alice to go away for a rest, but she couldn't. So, Monday I have a new help and I hope for the best. She is also Scotch. Both applicants were middle aged and seemed likely but the other did not look so strong and I want someone I am not afraid to ask to do things too heavy for me. Not someone I have to wait on. Mrs. Hassack certainly has got the cottage in nice shape. You'd never know it was *my* house. She had a passion for dirt demolishment. This one has a fierce eye in repose and I suspected red hair under the hat. It may mean "pepper" but she likes dogs. Mrs. Hassack has got very fond of the pups and fusses over them a lot. She has been a treasure for the month when I needed more or less nurse care. Now I can do pretty well for myself except washing my back and feet (bending and stretching). It is getting more difficult to realize the strangeness of not being able to attack things that I have always done. I sat on a stool today and pouted while Mrs. Hudson's boy planted some things I'd been given and came in tired as if I'd asked him to sow a ten acre field. It's ridiculous.

Am so looking forward to seeing you Easter. Don't expect to see a slim invalid. I'm fatter than ever around middle.

Just read a lovely letter from Mr. Hatch. I sent him a sketch at Christmas. A Metchosin one. He says he enjoys the reaction of the New York artists to it. It hangs over his desk. They all express surprise that it was done by a woman. They think I am lucky to live out here in surroundings in which one can grow and paint. They say there are too many distractions in New York although great stimulation in another way. Well, I do think I am lucky too. I have no doubt it would do me good to see more work and I often long to. But, there's always something new to see in the woods and glory in. I hope sincerely I shall be able to go to them again bye and bye. I like fresh goods not canned.

I had such a pleasure the other day. An old Vancouver pupil of mine (25 years ago) was over and looked me up. She was a young girl. Now she has two sons 20 and 18. She's a charming woman. Was Hazel Scott—now is Mrs. Gilmour. She took a paper sketch, "Pemberton Meadows," with her. Was delighted because, when she showed it to her husband, he said at once, "Why, that looks like Pemberton Meadows."

What with three visitors, gardening and interviews, I am tired, so will read your last two unanswered letters again and answer and close. Had an hour lying in the dark in the front studio. It is so nice having the double room. I often sit there for a spell.

Who is Mr. Band? Well, he is one of the Directors of the Toronto Gallery. Not an artist, but very interested in pictures. Lawren says he is discerning. Very difficult to decide—has had every picture Lawren ever painted hanging in his house at one time or another and then changes them. He has been very good to me. He is building a new room on his house and is taking "Nirvana" (two totems in a forest) he *thinks*. Anyhow, he paid $200.00 and is taking one of them. Won't hear any more from Ottawa till end of fiscal year, March, and goodness knows how much longer. You are entering Society of Fine Arts? Good! It is fine you are all working together and making a little group. I believe Mr. MacDonald[32] is very nice. I have met him twice, I think, but don't know him very well. Would like to see his work. Nan Cheney[33] is going to live in Vancouver. Her husband has a post in Vancouver General hospital. I know you will like her and she will fit in the art world.

How lovely about your car. I am glad you got one you really like. You'll have grand times in her, and I hope I shall ride in her some day with you. How did your talk go? Was it to the B.C. Arts? If you have a copy, do send it to me. Make your Victoria visit long as possible. Hope Fred is not a wreck with his rowing. It's fine *if he goes* to bed *early*.

Affec. yours, M. E.

---

32   *Mr. MacDonald,* J. W. G. MacDonald, at that time instructor at the Vancouver School of Art, later of Toronto.
33   *Nan Cheney,* Vancouver artist who often came to Victoria to see Emily.

316 Beckley St.
(October, 1937)

Dear Edythe:

Your letter and then one from Nan. Both about exhibition and both conflicting. Did not agree about anything. She thought it good—you bad, so I guess it was varied. What is Max doing? Did he get a school? His University classes are over aren't they?

We had a loathsome murder the other night—out Montreal Street. A poor old crippled woman on relief. Everyone is rampant. Of course, nothing is discovered of doer. Today is my bed day and I have written no letters. Was correcting some M.S., have done a little reading and some sewing.

Went to "Good Earth" Saturday. Saw it was on and took a taxi there and back and sat through it. It made me foam. It was so rotten. I was told I would weep but was not the least stirred. I *was* over the book. Did you see it? It was hideously American, not Oriental *at all*. No dignity—great hands and feet—Baaa— the only good thing was the oxen.

Flora bought me *Mornings in Mexico* by D. H. Lawrence and I liked it very much indeed. Little incidents. No sex. No dirt. Do you know it?

Margaret Clay was over to supper. She had a letter from Mr. Ayres.[34] He likes the stories but feels, like Dr. Sedgewick, that the public would not and they don't want to risk it. But he did give them very good words.

This week a day abed. Cuts into painting time though I will say I'm better for it. Miss Cann phoned today. Says she's com-

---

34   *Mr. Ayres,* Hugh Ayres of Macmillan.

ing to see me Wednesday but she's as threatening as thunder. Lismer did not look this way. Did you speak to him and his lady? Who got the medal? Nan liked MacDonald's things. I rather hope he got it. I hear he has gone to Hollywood? Lock, stock and barrel or just snooping? I kind of "expected" from you this a.m. but did not get. I wanted to hear about the party. Someone told me one of my things was reproduced in the *Studio*. I don't know when or why, who or how, or which and perhaps it wasn't at all.

Good-night—headache, M. E.

Hoping for a line from you. Lost this meantime. Miss Cann visited me yesterday. Came and had tea. Decent of her to come. She looks *so well*. Told me Evelyn Maynard in hospital for an operation. Said they took it casually but she thought it might be serious. I thought they were in Vancouver. Pouring wet for Pres. Roosevelt's top hat today. Too bad. Write soon.

Monday morning.
(Early November, 1937)

Dear Edythe:

While I am waiting for the stove man, I will begin to you. I had to write other letters yesterday and did not get round to you. Two to Africa for Christmas and one to England to thank a friend for *last year's* Christmas present that only came last week. Two pounds—which I am going to return for paints.

It is Monday, my bed day and such a blustery day. Wind raging, rain spasming, sun trickling, real wintry. Wow! Wish there were two summers to every winter. Maybe then we could bear it more sweetly. On Saturday I had some business at the bank and Florence Jameson[35] drove me in. We went to see stoves too as we were just sick to death with that hall beast. It was dirty and a sulker. Never was a success in this house—all right in the other. So, I got a plain, long box thing, the kind used by Indians and loggers. Solid iron. It will be much better I think in comfort and fits our hall only its door won't shut tight so the man is coming to wrestle with it. Oh! my goodness! Always something! Yet I should not be kicking at all because I have lots of luck one way and another. We are recuperating after the wrestle with the house and now they tell us we could have had it one year more. But, we are glad to be quit of it. Alice found it *very* trying. She hates the rent business and it fell on her, being handy. I did what I could but it was not much. Only phoning, advertising, and such.

I worked two days this last week and hope to get busy again. For five weeks I did nothing. The bother of the other made me too tired to want to work. Well, stove is fixed. Just a hole in the hinge not bored deep enough. Very good stove men. They bought up our old ones and are prompt and obliging which is rare to find these days.

We are not very rich from the sale of our furniture. We had not much of value and picked out the bits we wanted to keep. Both our houses are comforted with odd bits. I did not keep much. My house was full enough. Just the little old "what-nots," a couple of chairs and two tables and I gave one or two things of mine away to make room. I have the old dangling

---

35 *Florence Jameson,* at one time Emily's housekeeper.

doorbell. Willie fixed it up and put it on the door so when it opens, the bell rings like a shop, and I feel I should rush out and ask, "Soap? Candles? Sausages or shoes?"

I went out three times lately. One morning Humphrey Toms got his brother's car and took me to our old picnic place—Clover Point and we sat there in the rain and looked and smelled for a bit. I said I would rather sit than drive and it was lovely. Another time, Mrs. Cash[36] took me for a toodle around Uplands and Saturday, Florence took me to town. Gee! I hate town. Felt lost and got so weary and do so very little. It is hard to get parking and means you have to walk a bit.

No word from Dr. Sedgewick. I was going to write and ask for my things but hear he is still ill and away from the University so guess I'd better refrain indignation. I'm sick of them all. Ruth sent "D'Sonoqua" to Blackwoods and I've been writing the last seven months to ask her *who* she said it was to be returned to and she never answers. Then I wrote to Blackwoods and got reply that it was returned to wrong address last *May*. Too late to trace now. It would have helped a lot if she had answered my letters when she was in Duncan or England or France. So that is good-bye "D'Sonoqua." Well, I don't believe that anything will ever happen to any of them anyhow, so why worry. I only wish I did not *want* to go on writing.

Tomorrow Evelyn and Max are coming to have supper with me. She is better but not very strong yet, I imagine. I hope I shan't bite Max. Have not seen him in ages. Not all summer.

I am not sending over for the "Canadian Group" but using some of the stuff I have over there (the three Mr. Band took back). I could send *express forward* but I had already arranged

---

36 *Mrs. Cash*, Gwen Cash, Victoria writer.

and those three have not been shown in the East before.

How's work? Bring some along for me to see when you come. Do. What a bother to run Fred's lecture so close to Christmas. Better come for it and stay right on. Just think! Christmas again! The ages are made up of Christmases. Oh, well! Hi-diddle-diddle! There we go. How nice it will be to have a chatter with you again. Love to Fred. What's happened to Henry? I see that boarding place has gone. Lots and lots of love to you from

Your,
M. E.

316 Beckley St., Monday.
(December, 1937)

My dear Edythe:

You were lovely to answer so quickly and so nice and explaining and I learned a lot by your pulling out of memory the drift of what Dr. Sedgewick said. Yes—you did say he admired and was congratulatory etc., but that was not what I was after and wanted to know about. Perhaps I wanted to know more about the working side and wherein I could get ahead by being shown up my failings. I'm glad he does like them of course—very. I wrote to him after I got your letter and never peeped you had mentioned his speaking of them. I just wrote that it was a long, *long* time since I had sent the stories, I knew he was busy and maybe he was disappointed and did not like to tell me, in which case, they might as well come home and be forgotten.

He answered briefly that he was delighted with them, that

he feared they would not find a *big* appreciative audience but that they deserved it and he thought the next step was a consultation with Miss Clay (whether he or me, I don't know). He said that he had been very pressed for time and that *"criticism of this sort is not an easy business."* You know, that surprised me. I had thought of his reading and correcting like a school mistress doing the day's class exercises: Scoring out words or sentences and scribbling "bad," "clumsy," "unconvincing," and such like in the margin. I never thought of a Professor of English having anything but "easy business," when it came to beginner's work. I felt a bit ashamed I'd been impatient and given him extra when he was busy. I told him so and will just let the whole business drop, and when you go to New York, we'll dig them up if he has not lost them entirely by then. Anyhow, thanks to your letter today, I believe he thinks they are not twaddle so that heartens me. That was what I wanted more than anything to find out. I did hear some such dreadful twaddle when I attended Mrs. Shaw's classes and I was terrified mine might be the same. You *cannot* tell yourself.

I am distressed about your eyes and also about your work. You should have had a canvas for the show. *Don't get disheartened.* If you slog on and on, something is bound to happen. Lawren told me that, when I was in such purple despair in Toronto the first time I met him, and how many times I used to think of it, trying to work with those filthy tenants all round me, sapping the joy out of everything. I'll be even with them yet—using them for stories. So buck up and paint! You did not mention that Russian [Ustinow] I met at your tea. Never could remember his name. Are his pictures in the show? Is he still working? Good for Delisle. Mrs. P. said he was going to Forbidden Plateau to get big stuff. Lucky devil! Why aren't

Weston[37] and Max showing? Seems to me we are all slack. I was not proud of my own. I had some big ones but had to crate myself and had no box. We sent every crate that was sizeable East. Willie came next day and made one for Mr. Band's.

I am doing my "lying" today and I must say I feel lots better since the Doctor insisted on a complete day a week in bed and an hour every day after lunch regardless of get-up time. Take care of your eyes. Are you studying Russian *hard*? You will be eligible for an Ambassador yet, or court interpreter but, don't go to China—it's ugly; and do not anger your eyes. Poor old Alice! I should be ashamed to grunt when I can do so many nice things in my forced idleness and she has to rest her eyes an hour after school and she can't do a thing after dark but listen to her radio. Thank goodness, she has that. She's always patient and cheery and her school is very poor too.

What is egg tempera? You are sporty the way you try new things. After all, that is the thing to do to progress.

I had a supper party—first in months—Willie and Flora. Flora brought me a book by Eric Newton, *The Artist and his Public*. I am half through it. Lots in it, one way and another, but Oh! this analysis and ripping to the skeleton! Why can't things just *be*? Half the folks are too busy tearing to grow, it seems to me.

Tell me if you hear anything of old Lismer. I do not expect to. He's a leaky old blowbag and I gave him some "lip," or, really it was a slice of cold shoulder, before he went away. I had a note about Canadian Group Show from A. Y. Jackson (President). They still send me addressed to 646 Simcoe St. Makes me tired. They're such a bunch of slackers. I am not going to send over special as there are lots of my things kicking round the

---

37   *Weston*, W. P. Weston, a Vancouver artist.

East now. Possibly they will rake one up. What's got into us all? We're a nasty outfit (artists). Lawren was the man to head artists: "sympathetic," "high ideals," "hard worker." He was the strong prop under all the Eastern shows. Nice to all the artists and tolerant of all the work. He's a "big boy"—Lawren. Mr. Band says he thinks they are in America for good—in the University crowd—more sympathetic environment than Toronto for his work. Well, I must write to Ruth and to Carol.[38] My bed day is good for correspondence. Thanks for writing me, also for offer of *New York Times*. We'll see what will happen. Anyhow, I'm going on. Luck to Fred's portrait.

Affectionately, M. E.

Saturday, September, 1938

Dear Edythe:

I am beginning to crawl out of my fatigue. When those crates got off, I was too tired to take a long breath even. What a nice visit we did have—you and I. Nicer, I think for being a surprise. I hope you got Henry fixed up too.

What with letters from Ruth in Africa, from you in Mexico and from Jack in Paris, I feel quite as if I'd been travelling.

Have been very lazy these last days, though yesterday I did go to town. Took the streetcar to Spencers, bought material for some work aprons and a new dress top and will have some sewing to do. I was deplorably shabby and paint spattered.

---

38   *Carol,* Carol Pearson, who as a young girl took drawing lessons from Emily and boarded with her. Author of *Emily Carr As I Knew Her.*

Winter seems to have come. Such heavy fogs and cold too, and nothing to do about it but bow as gracefully as one can and settle down.

I wonder when the show (me and other) opens? I don't know. Grigsby[39] says Nan and MacDonald offered to help him hang it. Very good of them. Tell me how it looks—don't depend on Nan's having told me nor she on you having told me. In that way, I fall plop between the two of you and hear nothing. Do, each of you, give your own opinions. I wonder if my things will look dark and sombre on the walls? I had a letter from Kate Mather[40] in Winnipeg. She had seen the B.C. show as she went through Vancouver and thought it *very good*. Better than the one she saw in the East at Grange Gallery but, between ourselves, she is not much of a critic. Her line is *decorative* art. The picture she bought from me was the old French that I did when I first came back. B.C. done Frankish, not real B.C. sombreness. I wish I had asked more about your work when you were here. The time seemed to go so quickly. I wanted to ask you about your nude they turned down. What is it like? Male or female? Are you settling down to work with vim after the new ideas accumulated? I did not show you my birds either. I lost my prettiest last Sunday but he was brought back after three days from blocks and blocks away, without a tail and very dejected. And, his wife was in the middle of kissing another boy too. So the poor chap buried himself under the cedar boughs and sulked and found life disappointing.

Always affectionately yours,
M. E.

---

39   *Grigsby,* then Curator of the Vancouver Art Gallery.
40   *Kate Mather,* buyer for the C.P.R. She gave Emily large orders for pottery for sale in gift shops in the Empress Hotel, in Banff, etc.

Dear Edythe:

Yours yesterday. I have been awfully busy. Several canvases and a manuscript going and keen as mustard on all. The afternoon light is longer now too. Well, first you want an answer about Delisle. Well, as far as that muff goes, I would not turn handsprings to hang next to him but, if you want me to help out—sure I will. I don't know what canvases I may have on hand—so many were shown in Vancouver recently (so no good again)—and I have another big show coming off I believe but I could have sketches mounted, I expect, if they would do.

They have asked me to allow them to put on a "comprehensive" show of my work in Montreal—Art Association of Montreal—in Spring. I don't know when or what. They said "especially recent work" and, as you know, it takes epics to get stuff home from the East. He said Eric Brown (former Director of National Art Gallery) and Toronto Gallery had promised to – – whatever people do when they help one another. So maybe they will draw from there and not get too much from the West. Will have to wait to hear particulars. They just wrote to find out if I would let them have it. Very nice of them. I have never voluntarily exhibited in Montreal. Only stuff that has gone with other exhibits so it is very nice of them to ask and I feel honored. These Exes are good for one. A kick in the seat for slackness because they do mean work even if you have plenty on hand. There is always reframing and reorganizing.

Alice's cold is O.K. thank you. Nan's studio does sound nice and you like MacDonald's portrait. Don't blame anyone for not showing a portrait half finished. I never show my things and Nan did not show me MacDonald though it was on the way when I was up. Gee! I'd hate to do portraits and particularly Weston I think. I should feel his delight in himself and his bragging too horribly to be fair, I think. The other day, when he came here (and everytime) he talks of nothing but his artistic exploits. I wonder how MacDonald's murals will come out? He is such a good designer. I expect they will be fine. So glad he got the job (murals in the new Hotel Vancouver). Nan says there is jealousy. What a pity! Seems to me he is the logical man to do it. Rotten job, I'd think. Are your new quarters nicer to work in than the old?

Had daffodils given me today. It is coldish tonight but we have had no cold snap yet this year. Hope it won't come too late and do damage.

Shirley has taken up a stenographer's course. Perhaps it is the beginning of the end but, anyhow, you can't get through that in a week. I would not stand in her way. They are all the same. Think domestic work gets them nowhere though she says she is very happy here and I believe she is. Oh well, the study won't hurt her. She's smart enough too.

Goodnight! Love to both. Hope you get some work done while Helen is with you to housekeep.

Yours,
M. E.

My dear Edythe:

Well of all! I wrote you yesterday and thought you off my chest for a spell of days and here I'm writing again! I would have thought that Vancouver had had enough "Emily" without encoring the dosage. If it is just for that Hunter Lewis— no! For *you*—yes! *Show* if you want to. Go ahead and have a University Show! I thought the room up there is small. Will it hold them? No, Mr. Grigsby is very nice to co-operate—I am afraid it will give you a lot to do and you already seem to be so rushed. I hope H.L.[41] will help and not get some malady that will leave the heavy end to you. I scarcely know him, though, and I'm a *cat*. I leave the authority to you, and know you will see they are re-packed right—no padding—only cleats to keep them taut.

As to the *Province*. You know how I *love* write-ups. Let 'em do their *worst*. I don't care as long as they write *honestly* about the *work* and leave *me* out. I looked through photos and Shirley says this one is best as it was done for reproduction in a paper. It probably is the clearest and most suitable though rather smuggish. I only have that *one* van one and I know what they are. Never send your photos back so I don't want to risk that one of my van family. If they do send this back, I shall faint dead away.

I'm resting up—still a wee cranky, Shirley would probably say. Everyone was so good to me. "I liked myself and glad I came."

Shirley off to town so will post this. People are very good

---

41   *H. L.*, Hunter Lewis.

to me. I don't suppose H. L. is *quite bad* and I really wonder he doesn't leave me to wither unwrote.

Love,
M. E.

PS: Is this clear? Anyhow, it means: Yes, you can have show- if you want to. Me.

NB: How long for? Me.

PSS: Say whatever is fitting to H.L. Me.

Saturday (November, 1938)

Dear Edythe:

Got your card this a.m. and phoned Mrs. Morley.[42] She made such a fuss, I would not borrow her old film. Said it was her "prize" picture, refused outright at first, ended by bringing it round so grudgingly that I said no and Willie says they can take it off a small print and enlarge, so she is giving you a small print which you can keep. I must say, personally, I do not think that photo suitable. There is such a gang of people in it who do not bear on the subject or have any point as far as I can see for the article. It is a very personal picture but I'll send along the little print *if* Morley gives it me, for you to keep yourself.

Dr. Sedgewick wrote me a lovely letter. He saw the show on the last day. Isn't it *beyond extraordinary* selling six. Mr. Grigsby

---

42   *Mrs. Morley,* a frequent visitor to Emily's van while it was parked at Albert Head. She took a picture of Emily sitting in the door of the "Elephant," with Miss Morley and Joyce Maynard (Max's sister) in the foreground. (See *Growing Pains,* page 350.)

sent me a cheque for $172.00 this a.m. and there is still a little to come in on one or two. I could never have believed an exhibition of me would have met with such warm response. But, it is the way you and Fred have worked for me and I must say, Grigsby has been very nice about everything. By the way, what of Delisle Parker? Have you heard anything of his reactions? I have not.

I have had some such lovely letters which have touched me very deeply. So sincere and appreciative. It has all astounded me, and made me very happy and bucked me up to fresh efforts. I'm such a slow old devil now.

Matilda is very ill in hospital. Vet says he does not know. The house, Pout and Shirley—all of us are disconsolate. I felt her only chance was to go to the kennels and be closely watched. She's such a wee frail thing.

Shirley has a long day out today. She gave up her Sunday to bring me home last week and half her Thursday to take Matilda to the Vet and back, the day before we left her there. She loves the dogs and will do anything for them.

Nan sent me the photos of the pictures this afternoon. They came out well, didn't they? But, I tell Nan, if there is expense connected with them, I must share in it. Tell me.

Mr. Hood wants some pictures left over with him. I'm not at all keen as I hate dealers and besides, they charge a terrific percent—nearly 50 I believe it is. I don't price high (he wants sketches) and you never know where things are. Pottery selling through agents used to give me the pip. I never tried pictures.

The woman opposite has just had twins. On relief and two already! Pa has just scratched on my door to tell me that one weighs five lbs. and one six. Oh goodness! Have had very little voice since coming home. It shuts off at every occasion.

Well, it's after seven and I've had no supper. Shirley is out so I must get some bread and milk instantly. I feel emaciated.

Good luck to *your* show. It is so good of you all and Dr. Sedgewick to spout too. How is "pore" Hunter Lewis? I can't think what he'll find to say except my birth and death dates. Hope you are feeling better and won't find hanging me too arduous. Tell me all about it.

Love to Fred and yourself—
lots of it.
Yours, M. E.

PS: Will not close till Morley brings her photo but it's not my recommendation that you use it.

M. E.

Mrs. Morley hasn't shown up with her old photo. Don't bother with it. This is one Willie took and better in a way because there is not that whole squad of people who are really beside the point. I really can see no object in their having that van scene—that's nothing but a picnic party and quite aside from *work* which is supposed to be what the article is on and *not* my private life. Looking at the photo makes me very homesick for the old van. How I did enjoy her. Alice is very downhearted. Eyes giving much trouble.

My dear Edythe:

I am simply *overwhelmed* and my head turning clean round hind before on my neck, with all the nice things said and done. I'll be uppish soon. I am so glad for your sake and Hunter Lewis' as well as my own that the exhibition was a success and am glad that the students enjoyed it. Dr. Sedgewick has really always been *very nice to me* and Hunter Lewis too although why H. L. should be is beyond my comprehension as my behaviour has not warranted it.

And wasn't the London paper mention nice? Thanks for the clipping. What a world! What a world! And Matilda is better too and home from hospital and the twins across the way born and thriving. I am having a sewing bee next Monday to cover their hides.

I hope you are not too tired after all your exertions. Thank you so much for all you did. Seven sold, no less! Isn't that grand! Yes, I think it quite fair that the Gallery should get commission on sales. As for old Hood, drat him! it is a curse getting them back from him afterwards. Much easier if they come altogether in their crates. He can have: "Flung Beyond the Waves"—$50.00 and "Woods Edge"—$50.00 (no more) till Christmas or up to New Year if he wants and then they can come home. He cannot have those two small $35.00 ones. By the time he'd sliced his 45% commission, they would not be worth selling. I'd rather have the sketches. Am particularly partial to one.

I hope with you that Hunter Lewis chooses the *photo* rather than the painting, which does give me the pip but *don't tell*

Nan. One can't judge his own neighbor but, for a newspaper re-production, I say photo every time. If H. L. wants any informa-tion re work, I s'pose I could answer questions. The only date I know (about) is "born." I don't quite see how, having only seen me once in the dark ages, he can have anything to fill up on (and I'm quite certain I did not lay my life a blank before him then). Seems to me you'll *have* to help him or me. Otherwise, the stuff might be surprising eh?

Oooch! Winter! Nose-nippy in the mornings. Stormy nights and rain, rain, though for the moment it shines.

A million thanks for everything. Hope Helen is better, you ditto, Edythe, ditto the world (ditto it needs it). But I have no kick coming just now.

Always yours,
M. E.

Wednesday, (February, 1940)

Dear Edythe:

Glad to get yours. Yes, it is queer how, even after a short stay away, the dirt has accumulated and how *awful* one's house looks. Dirt everywhere—flowers gone to pot—floors look deplorable. One thing, it makes one feel quite chesty to see that they make a difference somewhere in life.

Thanks for cutting. It amazed me to hear my pudding face called *square* and belligerent:—

Oh woud the gift some gifted gae us

To see oursel's as others see us.

Well, about that Ruggles.[43] I'm sorry Edythe, but I was just beastly awful. She was such a total *fool*—I could have taken to my bed with pip. She stayed one and one half hours and did not have any idea how to even *ask* things leave alone understand. I told her about the work but said, "Now look here, I *won't* tolerate a lot of mawkish personalism. That's none of people's business."

"Oh, I quite understand," says she.

She walked off with my good photos of Ottawa and promised *faithfully* they would be back by end of week. Broke her promise. They're not back. I phoned. She said she was coming in to see me on *Sunday*.

"No," I said, "I can't see you." I wasn't going to have that spoil all Sunday.

So she came over on Saturday, late. Brought back those pho-

---

43   *Ruggles,* the reporter sent by Ken Drury, Editor of the *Victoria Daily Times,* to interview Emily.

tos Nan had taken at gallery, the first show. Those things were absolutely no good. Never could see why Nan insisted on their being taken. They were never used as they were too small and out of focus. I will be simply furious if that woman does not return the others. Then she sat down. (I took her into the cold front room so that she should not stay, but she pranced all over the house *unbidden*.)

"Now," she said, "I want some of your personal history."

"Well, you don't get it," I said. "I am *Canadian* born of English parents, and proud of the fact. That is enough for your confounded paper. The rest is my business. Good Day! I'm busy, etc."

I'm not very good today. Did not sleep too well and dreamed I was very ill and Helen (your sister) was nursing me. My bed had not been made for a week and she would get me no breakfast. I began to berate her, "Look at my bed." I took out of it all the clothes of the whole Hembroff family and flung about fifty hats off the bed. Helen only shrugged and, to make matters worse, brought in some of her friends and a squalling baby in arms and they shrieked and cackled in the corner of my room while I hurled hats and underwear and scolded and cried, and finally woke up.

Have done no painting. Have not felt equal to it. Have been finishing up tags of writing which has seemed to get ahead of me. "Woo" is all ready for her final type. I am going to do it myself. Flora is going to do the Biog. Ruth and Flora have both been over it and don't agree on their alterations, making it rather pin-sitting for me and I'm *sick* of it, and feel like a grand bonfire. We've had three grand bright days but cold.

Isn't war news horrible? A woman here yesterday with Anstie said she can't go back to England now. I should not think anyone would want to, but her husband is there, so that makes a difference. One dreads the spring, wondering what will happen then. Chamberlain warns we have not *started* yet. Well, when all ships are at the bottom of the sea and all gold spent, nations will have to stop. But, there will surely have to be a unifying and standing together. What a lot of geography wars teach one!

And now—you'll probably hate me about the *Times* and the *Times* will do a sniff on me (if it comes out at all, more than likely it will be another flop) so why bother.

Glad Fred is O.K. Hope your own cold is quite gone.

Affectionately,
M.E.

PS: Whew! Jack [Shadbolt] is going generous! He did not come to see me this time. Had a long visit from Joyce Maynard. Plucky girl.